THE
INSPIRED
MINDSET

*How to Inspire your Mind &
Completely Transform your Life!*

REBECCA BUKENYA

Copyright © 2015 Rebecca Bukenya

Published by Action Wealth Publishing

www.ActionWealthPublishing.com
Printed and bound in the United Kingdom.

ISBN-13: 978-1512323771

ISBN-10:1512323772

"Thoughts create your reality"

ACKNOWLEDGEMENTS

Writing this book has been a truly rewarding journey for me.

I am so grateful for all the gifts and opportunities that God has provided to me and continues to do so, on a daily basis.

I would like to express my appreciation and gratitude for all the encouragement and support given to me by all my friends especially Manj Weerasekera in making this book possible. I am truly blessed to be surrounded by an incredible supportive circle of friends.

I also want to express my extreme gratitude to all the amazing teachers so far in my life for providing me so many key lessons and distinctions that have allowed me to grow and for their wisdom and courage that has allowed me to find and live a purpose driven life.

Finally, I want to thank you the reader for making the decision to pick up this book and taking this step of investing in YOU.

I wish you all the best on your own journey and look forward to hearing about your successes.

This book is dedicated to two amazing women who have had a profound influence in my life.

My mother and my wonderful sister, Alice Jane Harwood, who taught me valuable lessons and values that have shaped my life.

TABLE OF CONTENTS

INTRODUCTION

Several years ago I realized that I wanted more out of life, but didn't know what that looked like or **how to get It**....

So I began my journey of learning and self-discovery. I have spent several years learning and have invested tens of thousands of pounds on my own personal development. I have had the immense privilege of training with some of the best leaders in the field of personal transformation. People like Brandon Bays, Dr. Deepak Chopra, Brian Tracy, and about eight years with Tony Robbins—someone who is considered to be the world's greatest performance coach.

As a practitioner of Neuro Linguistic Programming (NLP), I learned various approaches and techniques. Armed with my newly acquired knowledge, I employed many of these popular approaches from very well-known and popular courses, seminars and books, many often referring to areas such as limiting beliefs and the law of attraction. These techniques have helped me achieve many things and some fabulous results in my life. There was a mindset shift within me that said that if I wanted anything in life I went after it and I got it.

There is no debate as to whether or not the state of melancholy eventually affects us all in some form or other. However, it is how each person deals with this inevitable lack of inspiration that ultimately determines who they are and what they become. Often, we pay too much attention to our negative internal voice and too little attention to the positive aspects of our surroundings and what's working and what's good in our lives. We allow ourselves to take on negative thoughts and influences with such deep emotional intensity that they become imprinted in our psyche and casually dismiss any good thoughts and experiences that happen to us.

Now is the time for you to start that journey of conscious awareness, to awaken from the deep sleep of blind oblivion and begin to pay attention to the thoughts and factors that are impacting your day to day life.

The secret to getting the best out of this book is to find your own unique balance and take on those key distinctions, tools, and techniques that you feel are most applicable and useful to you. It is my hope that, through the pages of this book, you will discover success in that endeavor and learn to take control of your own destiny.

Manifest your Destiny

Making the most out of your time is an important step towards succeeding in anything you try to do. Still, the buck does not stop there. Indeed, you will find that the road to success is not paved with gold but instead is lined with sharp rocks of disappointment, reformulation, frustration, and, (if you do it right), determination. By understanding how to use your conscious and subconscious mindset with the correct structure and discipline so that they work together as a whole, you begin to navigate through these challenges— or anything—work in your favour.

In this book, you will be introduced to the fascinating science of *"The Inspired Mindset"* that explores how to positively manipulate the strengths and weaknesses of the human mind. By familiarizing yourself with the various incredible breakthroughs and by using the proven tools, effective techniques, and understandings of this science as outlined in this book to essentially reprogram your mind, you can learn how to manifest your own destiny in spite of any initial perceived obstacles or circumstances.

Discover your Personal Secret to Success

Why is it that some people succeed and others do not? Is there some secret that successful people know that still remains a mystery to the rest of the world? As much as I would like that answer to be "no," it is, in fact, a "yes." Successful people understand the mechanics of the mind and how to use it in their favour.

This book is designed to introduce and explain to you the structure and the mechanics of how your mind works so that you can start using it in your everyday life to get the success that you want. By the time you finish reading this book, you will possess the power to transform your life in ways you never before dreamed possible. The key is to take the action. Once you understand the **"The Sensory Perception Actuality Model" (SPAM),** start using it with immediate effect. Use it in your day-to-day life and you will start reaping the rewards. Now is the time to consciously transform your life into something spectacular. This is the tool that will ultimately help you design your ideal lifestyle, the life that resonates with your true destiny.

Consciously Transform your Life

Within the pages of this book, you will slowly uncover the most effective ways for you to finally put your destiny back into your own able-bodied hands, all the while showing you ways to take the control away from those negative forces that you may currently think are outside of your control. This is not a quick fix but rather a restructuring in the way you think, act, and feel about your day-to-day life. As such, the philosophy, tools, and techniques explored in this new science of *"The Inspired Mindset"* is brilliantly designed to give you the keys that you need to unlock your true potential.

Within these pages, you should be able to gather the information and insights you need not only to find the inspiration to finally make a change but also to gain the wisdom it takes to get it done. You will be guided through the consideration, reformulation, and management of your thoughts, emotions, and perspectives. It is my hope that this book makes things clear for you by adequately explaining the subtle nuances of a holistic mindset model.

Find Yourself

Through the breakthrough lessons outlined in this book, you will begin exploring the mechanics of the following aspects of yourself and your unique existence:

> *Spiritual*
> *Mental*
> *Physical*
> *Pass It On*

You will become educated on the Law of Reciprocity which will show you why each of the above factors, and your reactions to them, play such a huge role in who you are. Here, you will finally get the answers that you have been looking for, and when the smoke clears you will likely understand yourself a whole lot better.

Turn a Dull Past into a Bright Future

In today's modern word we are discovering fascinating things at the speed of light. We want things yesterday, and we sometimes forget about the importance of living in the moment. Despite the old adage, knowledge is _not_ power if you don't understand how your mind works or how to use it effectively to your own benefit.

In order to move forward, you must first learn to master your thoughts and emotions by understanding the nature of thoughts. You will discover effective ways to get rid of the negative programming once and for all that you have ingested over the years. This will help you to learn how to adequately change your past—at least in the way you think. This is what the principles of _"**The Inspired Mindset**"_ are all about. They will teach you how to turn your lackluster past into a brilliant future.

In order for us to erase the damage of our past, we have to be willing to do this while setting attainable goals that are in line with our life's vision. Training your mind for successful living is a vital part of being a happier and more fulfilled person. That's where _the tools and techniques outlined this book,_ and the scientific and holistic breakthroughs come into play.

Identify what you want out of Life and learn how to get it

All of the promises of the science of "**The Inspired Mindset**" might sound too good to be true, and you will find that such is the case, if you are not willing to put some effort into the cause. To make the science work for you, identification of your lifelong goals and the development of a workable plan are the first steps; both are vital in the process. This book will walk you through the process step by step so that you can get started on your journey of successful living.

Here, you will figure out how to develop a realistic and attainable life vision. Through various mental and emotional exercises and by giving proper considerations to outside influences, readers should be able to do the following upon completion of this book:

- Identify what you want out of life.
- Develop a workable, multistep, goal-oriented plan that is focused on how you will get to the finish line.
- Understand how to program yourself for success.
- Incorporate positive, repetitive habits, successes, and mindsets into your daily life such that you are constantly feeding yourself a good mental diet.
- Maintain your conviction to the cause.

- ➢ Manage your mental state in spite of perceivable challenges or circumstances.
- ➢ See your thoughts for what they really are and learn how to consciously control them.
- ➢ Learn how to ensure that your whole mind works with you to create and fulfill your goals
- ➢ Increase your self-esteem and compassion.
- ➢ Understand how to use the mind mechanics model to create success.

Join the other successful people who now enjoy a life full of joy and life satisfaction by using the scientifically proven tools and technologies described in this book to develop their life's mission and see it through. Each person will likely have a unique experience when working through the lessons and exercises that are described within this book.

Although there is research to back up all claims made, it is important to remember that you are a one-of-a-kind person. What you get out of this book will depend upon how serious you are about transforming your life and how much effort you are willing to put in. You should not expect the same thing as another reader, though your success stories will most likely be quite similar. Ultimately, you are the difference that makes the difference, but you must apply discipline and practice to the cause.

In reality, the proven research and the value of the science should make it easy for you to decide for yourself if the tools and techniques outlined in this book could actually work for you. Now is the time to make that change, and it begins and ends with you—resonating educated positivity and structured readiness from the inside out.

CHAPTER ONE
Grasping the Fundamentals of How your Mind Works (Conscious Awareness and The Nature of Thoughts)

Today is the day that you finally embark on a new journey in your life—one that will ultimately lead you to be the person you have always wanted to be. All across the world, people are struggling to find meaning in their lives while trudging through the trials and tribulations that come with just being alive. The lessons in life will never end, but you can begin to understand ways in which you can make changes when you grasp the fundamental principles and techniques explored in this book together with the understanding of the **Sensory Perception Actuality Model (SPAM).**

You see, life's troubles are not unique to your humble existence; truth be told, we all have hard times, and most of us deal with negative influences more often than we would like. The fact of the matter is it is not the troubles that get us down. In reality, it is how we deal with the truths of life that ultimately determines our demeanor, our self-esteem, and our destiny.

This book references the breakthrough tools and discoveries employed in approaches such as **Neuro Linguistic Programming** (NLP) techniques, **Self Power: Spiritual Solutions to Life's Greatest Challenges** and **Science of the Mind,** all revolutionary ways of thinking and acting that can transform your life. In order to get the maximum benefit from the practice, however, you will first need to understand the fundamentals or basics of the mind and how it works.

Part One: Exploring the Science of the Mind and its Benefits

Developed by Dr. Ernest Holmes, the **Science of Mind** technique was originally introduced to the world in the hopes that it would help people transform their lives from the inside out. Ingeniously designed to be very easy yet highly effective, it gives practitioners the freedom to make their own choices which ultimately allows them to manifest their ideal destiny in a way that makes sense to them. Through the use of various mantras, exercises, personal principle developments, the incorporation of new habits, and reconstructed thought-processes, those who understand and follow the guidelines of the **Science of Mind** (the basic philosophy of which is reflected in this book) are more likely to increase their self-esteem and forge a more satisfying existence.

The tools and techniques discussed in this book are focused on teaching you how to actively engage in your thought processes and emotions, both consciously and subconsciously. These tools, if applied, will help you to create change in all aspects of your life. Using these lessons, you will learn how to control and order your thoughts and/or meditate with conviction in order to heal yourself spiritually. As your self-esteem increases, you will also find it easier to express compassion and love for yourself and others.

"...A PHILOSOPHY, A FAITH,
AND A WAY OF LIFE..."

Those words are from the main creator of **The Science of Mind**, Dr. Holmes. ·He uses a morally-based belief system and combines it with an acceptance that we cannot always be in control; when mixed with a series of effective practices, it can help you to create the life of your dreams.

The basic law of nature states that "in order for anything to grow and thrive, it must also contribute to the environment in which it lives." Hence everything that you learn should be used on a daily basis. This will help grow your understanding and self-awareness. In turn, this will also help you develop a new way of life that is more in line with what you had in mind for yourself. The philosophy described in *"The Inspired Mindset"* is centered around understanding the following key principles:

1) Understanding Thoughts and Nature of Thoughts
2) The Power of Setting Outcomes and Clear Visualization
3) The Habit of Daily Success Conditioning

It is your willingness and ability to create and follow simple daily habits each day that is the basis of your success and the success of Dr. Holmes's research. By practicing each day, you will develop a better understanding of the ins and outs of your unique mental and emotional mental control center that is your mind. The philosophy of *"The Inspired Mindset"* is precisely what the New Age is all about—a rediscovery of who we truly are as spiritual beings.

1. Understanding Thoughts and the Nature of Thoughts

We create our experience through our thinking. Essentially, every thought we have is an illusion that we use to make sense of the world around us. Each of us experiences a subjective reality created by our thinking and interpreted by the beliefs, values and memories that are stored in our deeper or subconscious mind. This is clearly evident when two people who were present at the same event or same situation are asked to describe that event in detail. Evidence shows, that two people can experience a situation or event and yet have very different interpretations of that experience.

This can be easily explained by the fact that even though we all use the same five senses to experience the world around us, we have very different filters for how we represent that experience or event in our own unique mind.

The fact is that thoughts are things that shape our reality. Our experiences are created by our thinking, and everything we think creates an emotional stir within us. We know this to be true because, by simply recalling a frightening film we once saw, we can suddenly feel a sense of dread or fear that that memory creates. Likewise, if we imagine something that excites us, we feel a sense of elation or joy and sometimes a feeling of excitement or a feeling like a fluttering of butterflies in our stomach.

The average person is not aware of the thoughts that they are having on a moment by moment basis. Due to this lack of awareness, they fail to control their thinking. They do not know that they simply need to be aware and observe when they feel themselves slipping into a low mood or state which causes them to have these low quality thoughts. When our thinking is low quality, we feel a sense of uneasiness, a form of stress or tense anxiety or nervousness. In this situation, any attempt we make to think our way out of that state by trying to analyse our thoughts or work out the cause of our feelings only brings on more of the same thinking, which in turn creates more of the same feelings.

Solutions are difficult to be found in non-resourceful states of upset, anger, anxiety, or depression. When we feel ourselves slipping into a low mood, conscious awareness allows us to acknowledge and recognise that we are experiencing low quality thoughts. With this awareness, we can choose to be an observer and let these low quality thoughts go rather than engaging with them.

Every new thought is an opportunity for new and different more resourceful emotional feeling. When we choose to be an observer and allow our thinking to flow, we can relax knowing that our thinking will shift into a space of clarity and we will be open to insights. When we make decisions from thinking that is not coloured by feelings of emotional turmoil, we are more in touch with our true nature.

By understanding how thinking works, we are able to let our thoughts come and go, using our feelings as a guide as to which thoughts we need to focus on and allow into our deeper mind for imprinting.

When our perception of reality is distorted, we panic and lose the sense of our wellbeing. Conscious awareness enables us to see that thoughts are just tools. Hence with this understanding, we can use our feelings to monitor how reliable our thinking is in the moment. This in turn, then allows us to wait until we are calmer, see the situation more clearly before we take action.

With this conscious awareness and understanding, the nature of thought allows us to let our thoughts flow without having to practice doing it. With practice, this way of thinking becomes a way of life.

Once we understand that our thoughts are arbitrary tools and our thinking moves from low quality to high quality moment to moment, we learn that we do not need to pay particular attention to the thoughts that make us feel uneasy. If we have an issue or a situation that needs to be resolved and we feel any kind of anxiety or distress, we know to let go of the thoughts creating those feelings, safe in the knowledge that once that thinking clears, new thoughts and feelings will come along bringing new insight with them.

We only need to put ourselves in a resourceful state to get in touch with our innate wisdom which is deep within us.

2. The Power of Setting Outcomes and Clear Visualization

The highest intention of the spiritual principles that are clearly described within the **Science of Mind** structure is to give people the ability to anchor every aspect of their lives on the divine vision, achieved through developing and maintaining the power of visualization. So, what is visualization and why is it so important?

In order for a person to adequately visualize anything, they have to be able to travel within themselves, so to speak. Being in touch with your inner voice, whether alone or while participating in a group, is the best way to hear the callings of the highest source. Regardless of the activity, project, or relationship, affirmative prayer, mindful meditation, and clear visualization all work in tandem to help you manifest your destiny.

Often used by people who are new to the **Science of Mind** but also used quite frequently by people who are seasoned to the practice, guided meditation is a highly effective method for reaching a spiritual awakening. Through the use of suggestive methodology, guided meditation with the **Science of Mind** as the main catalyst can streamline the process of your becoming the best version of yourself. Although clear visualization can become rather simple for some people after adequate practice, the usual case is that it takes a while to make a noticeable difference.

The secret is to remain steadfast in your endeavors while being patient and having faith in the outcome. Guided meditation is not necessary in order to effectively visualize, but it does tend to help those who are less experienced or who have an exceptionally strong will. To expedite the process and to help you consolidate your overwhelmed mind and soul, ask yourself some questions before you sit down to pray, meditate, or visualize anything:

- What is the best outcome for this particular endeavor?
- What needs to take place for this to happen?
- What do I need to release to see my dreams come to fruition?
- What should I be embracing?

Understanding those questions is what will make the visualization process work for you. After a sufficient visualization session, participants are encouraged to journal about their visions, emotions, and ideas. When done in a group setting, there are often shared visions and feelings—a true testament to the value of the **Science of Mind**. Visualizations can be done as a solitary practice or alongside others, especially since it is often described as a "community spiritual practice."

The main concepts, principles, and exercises that comprise the **Science of Mind** are meant to help you recognize and follow the divine influence that flows in and around you on a constant basis. Through adequate practice you should be able to move through the motions of manifesting your destiny to express your unique vision and see your dreams come to fruition.

Unfortunately, this often requires a literal reprogramming of the subconscious mind, which can be quite difficult for a lot of people.

> *"Change your thinking and therefore change your life."*
>
> —*Dr. Ernest Holmes*

It is not always a simple endeavor to revamp the way we think. Most of the time, it requires us to dig deep into our subconscious mental control centers to pluck out the preprogrammed junk and damaging thought processes that lie hidden within. This obstacle, commonly known as lack of focused attention, is precisely what leads most people astray on their journey through life.

3. The Habit of Daily Success Conditioning

The daily practice of success conditioning is one of the key variables that separates the wealthiest among us from the poorest. Talent, aptitude, and charm are great, but more often than not it is the positive daily habits that we practice with discipline that bring about incremental steps of success. These subconscious, second-nature activities are in the driving seat and are what controls our waking hours. That means that for two out of every five minutes all day and every day, we operate on autopilot.

Armed with this understanding, would you not set up your subconscious mind so that it is fit for purpose?

Habits are neural pathways stored in the basal ganglia. This is the golf ball-size mass of tissue right in the center of our brains, within the limbic system. This neural fast lane is meant to save the mind energy.

When a habit is formed and stored in this region, the parts of the mind involved in deeper decision-making ceases to fully participate in the activity. Therefore, it makes good sense to prepare the soil that is your mental control center or "Autopilot" to ensure that it essentially has the right foundation and is fit for purpose for all your good thoughts to land onto and take root. This process is what is known as programming or imprinting.

This can be achieved easily and simply by you practicing success conditioning. This is simply a process whereby you replay a mental movie of all the successes that you've had during the day however small with emotional intensity.

Part Two: The Sensory Perception Actuality Model (SPAM) and How our Minds Work

From the moment we are born and some people believe even before that, our mind is always working and recording everything that it experiences from the environment around us. We all pick up information and react to the world around us through our five senses.

- **V**isual sense (or sight)
- **A**uditory sense (or hearing)
- **K**inesthetic sense (or feeling-internal and external-physical)
- **G**ustatory sense (or taste)
- **O**lfactory sense (or smell)

When something or an event happens in the external world, we have a thought about it (albeit in a split second) which is then filtered via the RAS for processing based on your beliefs, values, and past experiences or memories.

The RAS—which stands for the Reticular Activating System, is the automatic filter in your brain that brings relevant information to your attention. It acts like a bridge between your conscious and subconscious mind by taking instructions in the form of thoughts from your conscious mind to your subconscious mind. The RAS works by deleting, distorting, and generalising information; then filtering or breaking it down based on your personal beliefs, values and memories/experiences.

This internal representation based on our memories or personal experiences will cause us to have an emotional response and how we react to it. In other words, whatever is in the top draw of our subconscious mind is led out in the form of a response or reaction, which then becomes our reality.

For example:

- You see a spider (Visual sense)
- You have a thought, "Oh my God, a spider!"—(Thought in your Conscious Mind)
- What does that mean? (RAS—directs this to your Subconscious mind)
- Spiders bite (Memory stored in your Subconscious Mind)

- *Arrrh*!!!—You scream (Response or Reaction directed from your Subconscious Mind)

Key points about the RAS

You can deliberately program your RAS by choosing the exact messages that you send (in the form of your thoughts) from your Conscious mind to your Subconscious Mind, creating exactly what you want to come about.

For example, you can set goals, affirmations, and incantations or visualize your goals.

It was Napoleon Hill who said that, *"Whatever you can conceive and believe, your mind can achieve."*

The RAS can't tell the difference between what's real and what's imaginary, i.e., it will take on whatever message you give it in the form of thoughts. Hence, you are only limited by the size or creativity of your imagination or whatever memories you have in your top drawer filing cabinet—which is your subconscious mind.

So, in simple terms, all you have to do is create a very specific picture of what you want in your conscious mind and pass it on via the RAS to the subconscious mind with deep emotional intensity—which will help you achieve the goal. The RAS does this by bringing to your attention all the relevant information relating to the goal—which otherwise would have remained as background noise.

But equally, if what is in your top drawer filing cabinet that is your Subconscious Mind is not fit for purpose, the RAS would prevent your goal message getting through to the subconscious. Quite simply, whatever you focus on is what will come about. In other words, "**Thoughts create your reality.**"

This has been studied and researched especially in the field of "psycho-cybernetics"—the study of human mind mechanics.

The mind works like a guided missile and strives to reach the goals it has been instructed to target. This goal-seeking machine is a powerful tool and the best asset that we have as human beings that we can use in our efforts to reach our goals and achieve whatever we want in our lives. Hence, we need to learn how best to use this mind machine to our benefit.

This book will teach you strategies and tools of how to use your mind effectively to guarantee that your mind machine strikes those goals every time that it has been instructed to target.

Contrary to popular belief, as human beings we are not in conscious control of our decisions, not even the small ones. This, in turn, is what dictates how we act in any given situation. Unfortunately, we are not taught throughout our formal education the simple mechanics of how our mind works and how we can effectively use it to create whatever we want. Instead, we are told in a roundabout way that we are nothing more than our foremost thoughts and the actions therein.

The truth of the matter is there's much more to us than that. Our mind is our most valuable asset. It is always switched on, always recording all aspects of our lives and we take it and our thoughts with us everywhere.

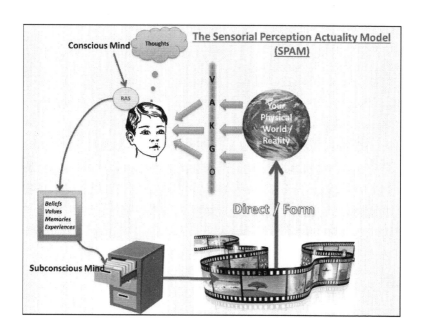

Essentially, our minds are designed to keep us alive. We structure our lives based on the things we perceive as we navigate through our life's journey. On the most basic level, we experience life through our five senses and then we store away those experiences and the conclusions therein for later. So, why do our minds do this?

Well, the answer to that question is rather simple. You see, our minds are designed to survive life through predictability. Simply put: our minds are prediction machines. When we wake up, we think about our experiences from the past and then use what we've learned (or deduced) to predict what we think will happen next. All of these thought processes are then stored neatly into a virtual filing cabinet in our heads within our Subconscious Mind. So, when it all boils down, it turns out that the first thought of the day is what ultimately dictates the direction we take and how our day (and life) shapes up.

Thinking about the positive aspects of your day instead of dwelling on the problems laid out before you can create two different realities. Truth be told, those first thoughts upon awakening are some of the most powerful ones. Those with any wisdom at all will say that knowledge is power, but more importantly, understanding how your mind works and how to use it effectively is the key to it all. On top of that, what you believe to be true is what your mind will keep and believe. So, if your first thoughts are about how much the world around you sucks, then your mind will filter through experiences with that mind-set as its main operating system.

In essence, your first thoughts determine how your brain will process the events of the day. If you start out negatively then your mind will tune itself into all of the negative that transpires. Your mind will be ready to highlight anything that disappoints for your viewing pleasure. After all, that is the station you switched to when you woke up. To put it plainly, what you believe you keep and whatever you focus on eventually becomes your reality or "**Thoughts create your reality.**" This is the fundamental secret to life that we are not usually taught from our peers or formal education!

The Denial of the Ages

Most people would like to believe that they are completely aware of their own thought processes, and moreover few would ever admit that their actions (and inactions) are due to some internal voice over which they have little to no control. Whether we like to admit it or not, most of us are not as aware of our thoughts as we think we are. In reality, we live our lives virtually oblivious to what our deeper thoughts and subconscious contemplations are telling us.

Doctor Sigmund Freud, the celebrated "Founding Father" of modern psychoanalysis, had some interesting suggestions on the matter. After conducting numerous studies, he found that human beings are more or less puppets of their subconscious minds. Even after the mystery was explored for over 100 years, modern neuroscience research is saying the same thing. In fact, the most recent studies carried out by the world's foremost neuroscientists suggest that our subconscious mind ultimately dictates our behaviours as much as 95% of the time!

This "underground chatter" and the "silent comments" that come from the depths of your mind are what drives your self-esteem or lack thereof. At the end of the day, it is this incessant internal conversation that eventually dictates your decisions. Understanding why this is important to your current mindset is the first step towards taking control of your destiny. It is no longer okay to live in the denial of the ages, but instead, it is time to wake up and start taking control of your destiny by taking control of your thinking.

We think about a lot of things: our homes, our family and friends, our careers, our love life, our hopes, our fears, etc. However, some of these subconscious thoughts are deeply ingrained into who we are as human beings, based on our past experiences or 'Former learnings'. Throughout the millennia, our species has acquired sets of survival and social skills that can be the basis of our day-to-day habits and behaviours. These deeply ingrained habits are also influenced by your cultural background or nature.

We all want to have a good life for ourselves and loved ones. We want more, but we are afraid to fail. This fear of failure renders us useless and leaves us paralysed that we are quite reluctant to even try. We tell ourselves that we can't have what is our biggest dreams because they seem like they are too far away. We say to ourselves, "Get real," when in reality, we are living in an unrealistic nightmare.

The Ninety-Five Percent

When the smoke clears and the mirrors are covered, your thoughts, emotions, behaviours, choices, and actions are all controlled by your subconscious mind. This is often referred to as your "Mental Control center" or "Autopilot." Despite what you may think or like to believe about yourself, you are actually at the mercy of your subconscious mind. If you think that for the majority of your waking hours you are in cognitive control of yourself then think again. Truth be told, your cognitive function is usually hovering around 5%. This means that for 95% percent of the time, you are running your life based on your subconscious mind or on "Autopilot" if you will. It is always in the driving seat.

The subconscious mind is where all our values and beliefs are also stored. So, if you truly believe on a conscious level that you can be successful, you are still only using about 5% of your mental power for the cause. If your wise Autopilot does not agree with you, then you will find yourself in some pretty hot water. You will be pitted up against the other 95% of your mind—the part that is saying you can't or won't follow through. Balanced beliefs, therefore, require the use of both your conscious and subconscious minds—aligned perfectly to move in one single direction towards what you want to achieve.

As mentioned, Dr. Freud suggested that we are little more than puppets of our subconscious minds. What experts refer to as your "principal learnings" or "conditioned responses" are central to all of this. These experiences are formed from past events, stored as memories, and reviewed later as you make decisions. So, if you set a goal in one area of your life and you work to consciously believe that you can achieve it, then you will most likely be a success so long as you have the backing of the deeper reaches of your mind. If not, you will be left relying solely on your willpower and conscious efforts alone (i.e., the 5%). We all know how well that works.

We kid ourselves into believing that we cannot succeed because we give too much of our attention to those thoughts and beliefs that it becomes our reality. There is a way around this though, and that is the basis of the philosophy explored within this book. Controlling one's thoughts is not always an easy task because, after all, these core beliefs are buried deep within our subconscious mind, which isn't readily accessible unless you know how.

Take being afraid of the dark, for example. There is usually no logical reason for a person to fear a lack of light, but because of our former learning/experience that we may have had as children deep-seated in the subconscious, we react whenever we are forced in that type of situation resulting in our reacting in a scared way. With practice, this too can be something that is erased from your life, but it does take some knowledge about who you are as a person on a fundamental level. In addition, you also need to have some skill at accessing your personal 'mental control center' or 'autopilot' so that you can better grasp why your mind functions the way it does and have the ability to consciously change it.

The Paradox of *Consciousness*

Regardless of the fact that the average person is constantly thinking about something, it is a given, according to recent studies, that people tend to use quite a small amount of their actual mental potential, especially for higher thinking. This does not mean that a person cannot achieve these higher and clearer states. With discipline in the practice of managing thoughts and emotions, pioneers and practitioners are beginning to learn how it is highly possible to access even more of their mind.

Your current mental capacity drastically affects every single aspect of your life. Your current level of thinking will not allow you to achieve your birthright. Once you realize and accept the scope of this fundamental fact, you will have a better understanding of just how your conscious and subconscious mind work together to formulate the person you are and the person you ultimately become. Being able to control this is the next step towards achieving your dreams.

For most people, the mind is never quite silent. We, as a species, are in a constant state of mental awareness. This can take many forms: stress, worry, anxiety, tension, fears and phobias, or even ambition. Those people who have been able to understand, conquer, and subsequently restructure their subconscious mind are typically found to have the greatest successes. This is not something that the average person can do overnight, but it is quite possible.

This is the secret to unlocking your true potential. _Think about it_: if you personally and deliberately program your subconscious mind to recognize and reach for a specific goal, your actions will mirror that. It is important to note, that the principles and science of **'The Inspired Mindset'** that is being discussed in this book is not simply an innovative thought process, it is a success-driven daily habit—a practice that you need to apply to your life with a focused mind. It is not designed to instruct you on what to do or think, but rather to guide you on _how_ to think, and eventually inspire you to act accordingly.

Part Three: Gaining Access to your Mental Control center

In order for you to benefit from the principles laid out in this book, you have to be willing to do a little work. There are three main steps to unlocking your true potential, all of which encompass the entirety of the concepts described within this book.

1. **Delving Beneath the Surface that is You**
2. **Believing in a Higher Power and the Divinity you Posses within**
3. **Taking Better Care of yourself to Fuel a Healthy Mind, Body, and Spirit**

Gaining access to your mental control center becomes a lot easier when you turn those practices into daily habits. There will be nobody knocking at your door to offer you a new life. The power is ultimately yours, but first you have to know where to find it.

One: Going below the Surface that is *you*

As discussed, the average person uses a rather small percentage of their mental power for higher thinking. Most of the time, we are busy contemplating our day-to-day lives, leaving us little time to really think about who we are or what we want out of life. It is not selfish to proclaim that you want more or want to live the life of your dreams. However, the first thing you will have to do is delve within yourself to find out exactly what those dreams are. Everybody is different, but luckily there are several ways that you could get this done:

- Mind Mapping and creative visualization
- Identifying what's most important to you in life or Lifestyle mapping
- Daydreaming
- Journaling and/or Free-writing
- Meditation
- Dream Patterning
- Hypnotherapy
- Psychotherapy
- Holistic Mind and Body Practices
- Chanting
- Guided Spirit Quest (usually with a shaman)

One of the most useful techniques or principle, and the one that is used the most within this book, is meditation. Regular and thorough mediation can actually alter the thought patterns in your brain, which could, in turn, change the way you act and improve the outcomes of your endeavors.

When you are in a fully alert and conscious state of mind, your brain function can typically be measured in mostly beta waves. Meditation changes all of that, putting your brain into an altered state of alpha, delta, or theta. Each of these has its own unique benefits to your overall wellbeing. Using stereo headphones and audible binaural or isochoric sound clips that are tuned to these particular frequencies, alongside your regular meditation, can help hasten the unlocking process and take you to deeper states of relaxation and consciousness.

Adequate meditation and contemplation is perhaps the most fundamental part of accessing your mental control center. For example, when your brain functions using mostly alpha waves, you have an easier time gaining insights with your conscious awareness. Most of the time, practitioners experience swift and profound waves of creative impulse—allowing them to come up with new ideas, even ones that may have been unrelated to the initial thought. In essence, unlocking your mental control center is what makes problem solving and innovation development a lot easier.

A much simpler method is practicing the art of being present or paying attention using your five senses in the present moment.

For example: If you are out for a walk, take time to really focus and notice:

1. The colours, brightness, shapes and sizes of the trees, leaves and things around you. Let yourself be immersed in this for a few minutes just using only your visual sense.
2. Then focus on just listening to just all the sounds around you, the pitch, depth and frequency.
3. Then using just your kinesthetic sense, feel the temperature of the air around you, the physical contact of the ground underneath your feet, the material of the clothing that you are wearing and how it feels against your skin; then also notice any emotions that you are feeling internally in this moment. (Are you exhilarated, excited, hopeful, happy, invigorated, etc?) Really drink that in.
4. Then notice any tastes in the air.
5. Finally, take a moment to notice any smells or odours around you or in the air and focus on them too a few minutes.

By practicing consciously paying focused attention to your surroundings using your five senses for a given period at a time, will help you in unlocking your mental control center. You may even find that you have insights and new ideas through this process opening up to new possibilities even ones that may have been unrelated to the initial thoughts.

Two: Believing in a Higher Power and the Divinity you Posses within

Nobody is going to come and tell you that you are perfect. We are all a work in progress, learning and evolving at a different pace. On top of that, depending on someone else to affirm your worth is a dangerous habit to get into. Once that person is gone or changes their mind, your self-esteem goes out the door as well.

To become a stronger and more resilient person, to gain access to your mental control center, and to ultimately live the life of your dreams, you are going to have to get real with yourself and start believing in the divinity that is within—bestowed upon you by the universe as your God-given right. At some level, we can all agree that there are forces beyond our collective understanding at work. It is this force that keeps you alive, allows you to breathe automatically, keeps your heart beating so many beats per minute and keeps your organs functioning in perfect harmony without your intervention. It is thought that this force, the "Higher Self," lives in the depth of your subconscious mind.

By awakening your mental control center, you begin to consciously work in partnership with that Higher Self allowing magic to come about effortlessly.

Being trapped in disbelief, tying up your energy on thoughts that do not serve you and majoring in minor things in life can wreak havoc on the conscious and subconscious mind. The key to unlocking your true potential is letting go and connecting with that High Power within you. This does not mean that you have to subscribe to some religion. What it does mean is that you merely need to have faith in something greater than yourself, while still understanding and respecting your worth, as well as acknowledging the impact of your subconscious thoughts and conscious actions on your destiny.

Fate = Instinct + Reciprocity

Your fate boils down to this: your instincts playing with the colours of what you have coming to you. If you believe in your own innate power—the divinity that makes you a sovereign and worthy person—you will unleash your ability to move through the trials and tribulations of life without feeling as defeated as you would have, if you started out feeling powerless. It is an inevitability that life is going to throw you some curve balls from time to time. To make the most out of the cards you were dealt, you will have to gain access to your mental control center and start making changes from the inside out.

Stop being a victim and slave of those ingrained beliefs and doctrines that have gotten you nowhere in life. The fact is, these were not yours in the first place anyway. They are learnings/experiences that you picked up along the way from other people's mind-set and beliefs. Beliefs that you picked up from your parents, school, teachers, peer groups, and the environment around you as you were growing up. Influences from the media, internet etc. that are not of your choosing.

How you performed in school, the outcome of past relationships, or your current physical state—none of that matters now. That is the past. Will you carry on as you always have? The choice is yours: Draw a line in the sand today, use the tools and techniques outlined in this book to unlock your true potential. Now is the time to start believing in YOU, and to begin putting that belief into practice.

Three: Take Better Care of Yourself to Fuel a Healthy Mind, Body, and Soul

If you thought of your mind and physical body as the most valuable possessions that you owned, would you act and treat yourself differently? Imagine if you thought of yourself as one of the most expensive high-performance cars such as a Maserati or Lamborghini. I bet you would treat yourself differently. For all intents and purposes, the average person is just like a Maserati. In order for that fine car to hit the road and make it to its destination, it will have to be filled with top-notch fuel and given regular oil changes and topnotch service. The same could be said about your mind, body, and spirit. All these three aspects of you need adequate attention, and forgetting to take due care and attention to either one of them, can make you sputter out, especially when you really need to hit the gas. After all, the component parts that make you unique as an individual like thinking, performing, planning, functioning, achieving, and dreaming all need careful nurturing.

If you want your mind, body, and spirit to function as a whole entity on a level that is conducive with gaining access to your mental control center and ultimately leading you to your fate, you will need to start taking better care of yourself.

Things that make a person happy are:

 ➢ Gratitude for what they already have
 ➢ Something to love
 ➢ Something to do
 ➢ Something to look forward to

Although all of those things are important, being a truly whole individual who is in line with success takes more than simply being happy.

Start each day by simply being grateful for who you are and what abundance you have in your life. The simple acknowledgement of the gift of being healthy, alive and loved can change your whole focus and outlook on your entire life.

A healthy lifestyle should be one of the most important areas of your everyday habit and focus and should not be taken for granted. There have been countless studies performed on the connection between what we eat and how we think. On top of that, our physical states play a huge role in how our minds function as well. Taking care of ourselves becomes something that is more important than vanity. When you really understand this at a deep, knowing level rather than an intellectual one, you truly understand that taking care of yourself affects your ability to succeed.

Getting plenty of exercise is important to your overall health, but it can also positively affect your ability to relax properly and benefit from your meditative practices and/or the other principles described within this book. The quality of food is also very important. Maintaining a healthy and organic diet is essential here, especially considering the effects that additives, preservatives, gluten, trans fats, and other processed "junk" has on the body and mind. For maximum mind benefit from your diet, try to eat foods that are rich in the following vital nutrients:

- *DHA*

- *Omega-3 Fatty Acids*

- *Super foods rich in Antioxidants (e.g. Chia seeds, Blueberries, raspberries etc.)*

- *Vitamin C*

- *Vitamin E*

- *Protein*

- *Good fats (e.g., organic raw coconut oil for cooking, virgin olive oil on salads, avocados, Brazil nuts, almonds, etc.)*

Keep in mind that there are numerous other important vitamins and minerals that you should be consuming on a daily basis. It is best that you talk to your doctor about your specific needs. What it all boils down to is this: the secret to transforming your life is adopting a new mindset. That is to say, learning how to gain access to your mental control center and changing your life is no big secret at all. It merely takes a willingness to acknowledge the importance of proper mind, body, and spirit functions and a discovery and an acceptance of who you truly are from the inside out.

Once you realize and accept the fact that you are an incredible person with a wondrous mind, you will be able to tap into your true potential and change your life for the better once and for all. There is no better time than the NOW to start restructuring your life to mirror what you see in your dreams.

CHAPTER TWO

The Holistic Mindset: Discovering our True Nature

Now that you understand the basics of the SPAM system you can start to use what you know to develop a holistic mind-set. This fundamentally organic thought process is what will ultimately lead you to success. Once you find yourself more comfortable with the finer points of your consciousness you can then embrace a holistic mind-set and thereby allow the colour, music, and life into your unique existence.

At this point you should have an unshakable respect for the subconscious mind and its powers on your decisions and emotions. You should know that the collective influence is rather strong, and thus you should understand the importance of opening up your mind to allow life to flow through your consciousness. Indeed, this is what your mind is designed to do. Remember that we think "for" our minds and not "with" it. Essentially, what's going on under the surface is beyond your control unless you rewire yourself from the inside out.

Now it is time for you to learn how to consciously transform your life by manipulating your own subconscious thought processes. Being able to do so takes some discipline, practice, a little patience and a lot of determination. It also requires that you learn some practical techniques and perform some exercises that are designed to facilitate this change.

Living life as a stranger to yourself is no way to exist at all. Developing a holistic mind-set is the best way to discover your true self and eventually get in touch with your destiny. If you continue on the path you are on now, as a slave to the 5% of your mind that is considered consciously awake, then you will never know who you are deep down. What a shame it would be to never familiarize yourself with your own true nature because you did not know how to develop a holistic mind-set.

From this day forward, if you take on a holistic mind-set, you will set out on an important path—one that will show you who you truly are and give you the power to do something about it. This is precisely what you need to turn your dreams into reality. In light of all the inevitable ups and downs of everyday life, a holistic mind-set will show you how to turn uncertainty into confidence and opportunity.

There is no debate that all of us have our own unique story to tell. It is those experiences that ultimately make us who we are. Still, at some point those ingrained beliefs might eventually clash with those of others, and thus we see conflict. Fortunately, it is the well-honed ability to develop a holistic mind-set that leads mankind to the ability to resolve these conflicts and thereby progress as a whole.

When we understand that we all have places where our beliefs are not 100%, we will be able to understand and benefit from the universal knowledge that is contained within that realization. On top of that, allow you to be more accepting by practicing a holistic mind-set which allows you to easily put down your personal walls that you have built over the years, which in turn will allow others to coexist with you in a mosaic of beautifully inspiring influences. In this way, we can all learn how to turn the unavoidable chaos of the world into a means through which we foster positive personal and worldly change.

In addition, a holistic mind-set also helps you to succeed without seeming like a pushy or judgmental jerk. It is when we learn how to accept the fact that knowledge exists outside of our usual sphere of knowledge that we can begin to benefit from the change in the form of co-creation and independence.

In order to achieve anything in our lives, we cannot walk around being afraid of change. Developing and adopting a holistic mind-set requires quite a bit of change that is all positive and designed to help you turn your dreams into a living reality. Changing the way you think takes a lot of practice, so you shouldn't expect anything overnight. Be patient and walk the coals to your destiny, keeping a happy and healthy holistic mind-set in the process.

What is the Holistic Mindset?

Understanding what a holistic mind-set is becomes incredibly important once you make up your mind to develop it. Essentially, a holistic mind-set is an organic and awakened way of thinking, acting, and being on a daily basis. As entities of this plane and time we all have life inside of us: we breathe, we walk, we talk, we think, we exist. However, the great debate between nature and nurture rages on, as modern science is showing how the location in which we are born plays a significant role in the outcome of our lives. It turns out that our behaviours, beliefs, and values are mostly formed as we experience and learn things from our peers and surroundings. As a consequence of these influences and experiences, we gradually turn away from our true nature.

Adopting a holistically healthy approach to life means that you acquire your sense of well-being from within. It cannot be accomplished through taking medications, undergoing surgeries, or buying items. Only you can summon what it takes to make those positive changes in your life, using outer influences as the inevitable yet potentially helpful catalysts that they are. Perhaps the best part of it all is that you will eventually come to the realization that you are already a vibrant being who is quite healthy in many ways.

Being generally healthy is one thing, but remember that you are a whole lot more than just a body that is hauling around parts until it wears itself out. Committing yourself to a holistic mind-set means that you also honour effective holistic health practices. You learn how to take small but meaningful actions so that you can reach the top of your own personal success ladder. In essence, a holistic mind-set and a related approach to your health will teach you how to move your ideas from thought into action, from action into habit, and ultimately from habit into your rightful destiny.

Self-affirmations are a big part of adopting a holistic mind-set. Although the element of truth is important in all situations, being proactively positive can lead to great things. Since a person's sense of health and well-being comes from within and then eventually translates to outer health and well-being, developing and practicing a holistic mind-set can transform your life in ways you never thought possible.

It is essential that you fully understand how the holistic mind-set really works before you put it into practice. It is an expression of life, instead of an intervention upon it. For example, when you take medications or have surgery to make yourself feel better you are not using a holistic mind-set. In fact, it is probably the absence of the holistic mind-set that got you in that situation in the first place. But when we use a more holistic approach to our health and our lives, we are more likely to avoid some of those problems from ever happening and then have a better ability to heal ourselves later on when the inevitable takes place.

Remember that a holistic mind-set and an approach to health that is in conjunction with it can change your life in drastic ways, but it all begins on the inside and works its way out. Taking a holistic stance to your own wellbeing means doing things because you are in tune with the greater meaning of them, and then truly appreciating those captivating things enough to literally feel the beauty of it in your bones. In other words, a person with a healthy holistic mind-set would eat deliciously fresh organic foods not because they wanted to prevent cancer or lose weight but because they understood and appreciated the natural divinity possessed by the food, and thus they would feel more connected and alive just by eating it. When all is said and done, it is our thought process that ultimately dictates how we feel on the inside and how we project those feelings on the outside.

Adopting a holistic mind-set is essentially the same thing as having a choice between fighting and thriving in life. When you use the thought processes that you will continue to learn from the development and use of this way of thinking, you will be able to implement it into every aspect of your life and turn everyday activities into opportunities to better yourself and reach your goals. When you practice mindful yoga, get a relaxing massage, shop for delicious food, go on an exciting adventure, or work out your body, you begin to use holistic thinking as part of your arsenal—replacing dangerous medications, unnecessary surgeries, and most of those other invasive "solutions" with something healthier and more beneficial.

Just imagine how much this newfound ability will change your life. Doing things because they help you prevent problems is one thing, but doing things because they make you feel good is another, especially when the practice is good for your health. The key to developing a healthy holistic mind-set is to walk the fine line between intervention, prevention, and reverence for the divine in it all. This myriad of colour, opportunity, and emotion will turn out to be the masterpiece that is your true nature and thus your destiny.

However, holistic living is incomplete without the social aspect. In order for you to create a supportive environment for your own wellbeing, you are obliged to share the good news with other people. By applying the mind mechanics model and following a holistic lifestyle, you will find that other people will be naturally attracted to you and aspiring to be you, wanting to know how you are able to create such amazing success in your life. Your role and responsibility is to share the **SPAM** model with them and how they can use it to make their own lives successful too. In this process, also take the care and attention to draw out the goodness inside of other people, so that they too start to bloom and light up from within. By giving genuine compliments, mentioning all the great things that they are good at will make them shine brighter and strengthen your own inner presence.

What is our true nature?

So, what is all this "true nature" stuff that keeps getting mentioned? Well, there are actually two portions to the average person's consciousness:

1. *What we call our "normal" or "waking" selves, consisting of our logical/conscious mind.*
2. *The Higher Self, which encompasses the subconscious mind.*

It is this higher self, *the greater mind*, the part within us, which gives us all life (or at least the realization of it). The part of our consciousness which acts automatically to beat our hearts, make us breathe, or allow us to blink without thinking about it all lives deep within our subconscious mind. By the same token, this busy portion of your true self is what stores all of your experiences/memories and then carries out any and all instructions regarding your reaction to them. The greater mind then directs these unique thoughts in such a way to create the life we experience and the beliefs and values we eventually hold.

Consciously understanding this concept can drastically transform your life if you know what to do with it. This fact is mostly because once you understand how everything is connected you are more easily able to use it to consciously design exactly what you want. As we have seen, everything we do, think, and/or say is automatically recorded. The greater mind, doing what it does best, then uses that gathered information to form thoughts and lead your impulses throughout life. Therefore, those who wish to change their conscious minds then begin to control their thoughts, actions, feelings, and words, thereby living life fully in the present—moment by moment.

CARELESS TALK CAN INDEED COST LIVES

Every one of us has that part of us that is tethered to the past—a portion of our consciousness that is constant and unchanging. Despite your conscious attention, this true self will eventually shine through whether you like it or not. We are all beings with survival in mind, so we can sometimes come across as harsh or unforgiving. Because of this, we should always pay close attention to what we think so that it does not become what we say, mostly because what we say eventually becomes what we do and our actions can cause drastic changes to our lives and those around us.

It is true that you are only responsibly for your own life, but that is not the end of the story. However, because you are not in this world alone you are also responsible for the lives of the people around you and those you come in contact with, which basically means that you are responsible for the entire world. This may seem like a lot of weight to put on your shoulders, but this becomes less overwhelming when you realize that by controlling your thoughts and actions you can thereby control your reality. If the whole of humanity were able to collectively understand and do this, the world we would be living in would be very different indeed.

Most people are blissfully (or miserably) unaware of the two distinct parts of the mind i.e.: the logical conscious normal self and the higher subconscious or deeper self. In response to this, the average person's mind is split in an effort to consolidate the confusing stimuli it receives. What results is a society filled with fragmented minds that exhibit schizophrenic behaviour while being slaves to a mysterious consciousness (also commonly called the "Matrix"). Luckily, the holistic approach to thinking is designed to make these two separate but equal parts of the mind whole again.

Becoming consciously aware of the deeper "greater" mind is of the upmost importance. It is the awareness that the mind has its own creative, life forming and intuitive capacity that allows us to create the life we want. This realization is the first step towards embracing a whole-life holistic mindset. In essence, this understanding is what allows you to imprint or learn only what you want onto the deeper mind and then see that very thing come into reality through conscious practice—basically overriding your normal tendencies to create a character that is more in line with your true nature.

Discovering and then maintaining a familiarity with your true self is vital to living a healthy and holistic lifestyle. Just as a person who works to stay in great shape fuels their body with the healthiest foods, you need to feed your mind the best thoughts while exposing yourself to positive influences. Understanding that your deeper mind is always switched on and always recording what you see, hear, feel, and sense is perhaps the most essential bit of knowledge to have when trying to discover your true self and live to the best of your ability. Acknowledgement of this knowledge and understanding alone is a major breakthrough.

"Health is a state of complete physical, mental, and social well-being, and not merely the absence of disease or infirmity."
—World Health Organization (WHO)

From this understanding, you will begin to act differently by ensuring that you do not expose yourself i.e. your mind to any stimuli that would damage its well being. You begin to think and say only good things to yourself and others. You begin to create a supportive and healthy mental environment. You spend time only with people with similar mind-sets, i.e. individuals that practice a holistic lifestyle and value growing and nurturing that inner presence or higher power within us all.

You need to know that embracing a holistic mindset does not stop with you. Of course it is important to respect and love yourself as a unique individual but you should also be aware that you are part of society. As a citizen of the world, you hold a responsibility to all of mankind. You are obliged to share the SPAM model and show and tell others how to use their deeper minds. To put it plainly, you must be that living example of what it means to live in a holistic way. Doing so is what will enable your own inner presence to grow, which means that you inherently benefit as well. The stronger your inner presence the easier you are able to work in creative partnership with that 'Higher Self' thus generating success and results faster for you. By sharing the model with other people, they too start to harness the power of their deeper minds as well, thus growing the collective subconscious. This is what will ultimately impact the world for the better. Essentially, in order to live a truly holistic life that is line with your true nature you will want to continually complete the circle and pass the goodness on.

This flow is indeed the very movement of life and evolution itself. Each person becomes consciously aware of their higher self, using the understanding to pass the knowledge forth and positively transforming the world—one person at a time. As a result of this, the consciousness of the entire planet is thereby raised, as more and more people connect with life in a more profound way. This, indeed, is the essence of what "true nature" really is—the ultimate source of creation and personal power. The nature and aim of the higher self is to evolve. It's a perfect, loving, intelligence, whose aim is to give you everything that you want and make the best better. Therefore, it has a vested interest to ensure that each one of us awakens to our true nature. The more you work in partnership with the higher self and help others to awaken to their true nature the more success and abundance it helps you create.

The higher self, the source, the part that gives life, the true self, they are all one and the same. This natural and inherent part of you is perfect, loving, intelligent, intuitive, sensitive, compassionate, and brave. Allow your consciousness to do its job of taking care of you, giving you abundance, and foster greater success and fulfillment in life.

Consciously Transforming your Life

There have been a lot of literary works that have focused on teaching a person how to consciously transform their lives. However, many of these books have not centered their approach on the scientific end of things. Thanks to newly adapted technological discoveries in addition to some pretty forward-thinking holistic minds, the proof is now available for anyone to find. In fact, one of the most popular modern books, written by Napoleon Hill called *"Think and Grow Rich*[4]*"* offers a simple yet powerful message to enthusiastic readers with a very sound scientific backing.

Although there have been several attempts by numerous experts to explain the phenomenon, consciously transforming your life merely requires a restructuring of thought at a subconscious level. In short, you have to teach yourself how to conceive an idea, and then you have to believe that it is possible for that you can finally achieve it. It may turn out that the task is easier said than done, but at the end of the day few things worth doing are ever easy.

Conceive, Believe, Achieve

The concept of conceiving, believing, and achieving should be an easy one to understand and a fairly simple one to implement into your daily life. These strange words and concepts may seem foreign to you now, but in reality they are all part of your true nature—the part of you that has been hidden by generations of misinformation, oppression, and confusion. Form follows function, so you will want to transform your thoughts to function as calibrators for your destiny.

To know how to do this, you will first need to understand the differences between conceiving and believing. The gap may seem clear enough to most people, but some people seem to have a hard time separating the two, and thus they fall into a rut that is dictated by their inability to formulate an idea and stick with the plan. In order for you to consciously transform your life you will need to do your homework on the matter.

Conceive: *A very easy concept to grasp in regards to the magic formula for success and life transformations. To conceive something means that you form an emotion, opinion, idea, or purpose in regards to some experience. Think of it this way: we all dream of a perfect lifestyle that is full of fun toys, fulfilling relationships, and happiness. We all conceive things every day. In fact, it is a vital part of logical and creative existence and it is a huge part of conscious thought. Conceiving is just the process of imagining or day-dreaming of something.*

Believe: *A trickier part of the magic formula of life transformation, the belief is essentially the glue* *that holds all other concepts in the conscious and subconscious. Try to keep in mind these wise words: "Whether you **believe** you **can** or **believe** you **can't, you're right**." What that means is pretty simple. The key to making real changes in your life is to structure a mental control center (or subconscious mind) that is fit for the purposes you aspire to. Mostly, what we believe is something whatever was placed in our subconscious.*

In order to consciously transform your life you will have to *conceive* a positive existence while *believing* that it is possible. As with everything in life, finding balance is the answer. Remember that reality always follows thought, which basically means that now is the time for you to start thinking about who and where you want to be.

"Thoughts Create your Reality"

How many times have you really believed in something yet failed to see it manifest into your reality? Most people could count on both hands how many times simple wishful thinking has left them, well... empty-handed. It turns out that neither sheer conception nor belief alone are enough to see any real results. By the same token, it is nearly impossible to transform your life without them. Because of this, it is important to understand how the mind works so you do not allow your mind to fool you.

This understanding is incredibly critical to your successful transformation. The mechanics of the mind as an area of knowledge requires deep examination in order for the majority of us to grasp the fundamentals of how it works. When you understand the process of how we naturally behave and believe as human beings will you be able to affect the properties of it at your will.

How many times in your life have you wished for something that is useful?

How much more effective would your hard work be if you were tuned in like this?

None of this is any whimsical, New-Age mumbo jumbo. It is all based in scientific fact. It would be nice to take the easy way out and believe that we are not responsible for the negative things in our lives. However, the reality of the situation is that we can consciously transform our lives, and it merely requires a habit of keeping the right thoughts. It is not brainwashing or mind control, but rather, it is a discovery of your true self while having a reluctance to deny opposition, all with an understanding that thought creates all of the life you see before you. Every great invention that you see today started as a thought in somebody's mind. Be it your smart phone, the internet or the clothes on your back. The mind is a wondrous tool limited only by the size of our imagination.

The Science of it All

Scientists have been speaking on the matter for quite some time now. The celebrated founding father of psychoanalysis himself, Dr. Sigmund Freud, made numerous observations regarding the subconscious mind and its ability to affect conscious reality. His work is what a majority of modern psychology and holistic thought is based upon; and although some of his work is quite controversial, those who have an appreciation for their forward-thinking peers would see Dr. Freud's methods as groundbreaking rather than precarious. Regardless of his reputation in the field, his innovative suggestions (namely that we are all merely puppets to our subconscious minds) has outlasted the test of time.

Over 100 years after Dr. Freud's last delved into the human consciousness, the latest neuroscience research is agreeing with his once scoffed-about theories. Recent studies carried out by some of the world's most notable neuroscientists actually show some pretty interesting data. Interestingly (or expectedly, depending on which side you're on), Freud was right all along. It turns out that your subconscious mind ultimately dictates every last one of your conscious behaviours.

In fact, your subconscious mind is responsible for your beliefs, values, behaviours, and/or actions at least 95% of the time. In simpler terms, your mental control center does it all. Your mental control center or

"Autopilot" is at the wheel for most of the ride, taking care of the important "life" things like:

- *Thoughts*
- *Emotions*
- *Feelings*
- *Behaviours*
- *Choices*
- *Reactions (or lack thereof)*
- *Involuntary body functions*
- *Beliefs*
- *Values and morals*
- *Tastes and Preferences*

Despite what you may think, what you know about yourself—those things that you believe, what you like and dislike, and so on—are all ruled by your subconscious mind. If you continue to think that you are in conscious control of yourself during the majority of your waking hours, then you are sadly mistaken. The fact of the matter remains: 95% of the time you are running off a subconscious autopilot that is filled with preprogrammed information, some useful for survival and success and some not so much.

On a purely scientific level, your subconscious thoughts seem to be running the game. However, you can consciously transform your life if you really believe that you can be successful at something, and if you hold that belief on a continual, subconscious level, such that it becomes a way of life for you or a conviction.

When you conceive a belief or vision about how you would like your life to be, you are basically up against a large portion of your consciousness. If what you try to imprint onto your mind does not concur with your higher self, it will definitely cause some opposition, mostly because you will be telling yourself that "you can't do it" or that "it's impossible." Belief therefore, requires both your conscious and subconscious mind to be congruent and completely aligned with what it is you want to ultimately achieve. When you think about it, transforming your existence essentially only requires about 5% of your mind power, since the other 95% is given to your already busy subconscious mind. However, since it is the 95% that is in control, you need to ensure that the subconscious mind is fully fit for the job at hand. In short, it has to have the right foundations in the form of programmes, beliefs and values, so that the instructions that you send it in the form of thoughts land on the correct fertile soil in order for them to grow and flower.

Remember that stored within your deeper mind are experiences, memories, and prior lessons that you have gained along the way. Thus far in your life, everything that you have been through has led you to this point. Your autopilot has essentially guided you in one way or another to these immediate circumstances. Now is the time to take a look at how these things affect your beliefs and values so that you can restructure things to your liking based on your newly discovered true nature and understanding.

If your true nature and your beliefs are not aligned, then it becomes extremely difficult to achieve any goal in any particular area of your life. It is a lot like swimming against the tide: usually pointless and always tiring. Some of the events in your life can have such a huge impact on the way you think and believe that they can drastically affect your life in several ways simultaneously. These instances can either make you or break you. Unfortunately, most people end up being in the latter group because they were unaware of how to transform their lives. They don't know about the **SPAM** *model* or how their mind works.

On the other hand, there are people who take control of their lives in ways that virtually turns everything they touch into gold. Those types of people are predominantly thinking at a deeper subconscious level—one that is aligned with the positive and productive goals that they have set. This increases their chances of success by exponential levels, allowing their sphere of possibility to take a quantum leap in the right direction.

Never forget that those deeply ingrained impressions that are currently on your mind, both positive and negative, end up being the fundamental controllers of your destiny. Oh, and you remember the other part to that conceive, believe equation? Yes that is the **Achieve** part. Once you are able to grasp how important to have the right beliefs and values, the **Achieve** part, then becomes very easy.

You can achieve by simply modeling other people who have created the successful results that you want by applying the same strategies and tools that they used and simply applying them.

However, this all hinges on step 2 the **Believe** part. Understanding ways to do this is what will make it easier for you to attain the goals that you aspire to.

Exercises for Success: Developing Personalised Methods that help us discover our True Nature

When the right conditions exist on a conscious level, you can literally reprogram your autopilot. This will eventually give you the correct alignment, so-to-speak. Both parts of your mind, the subconscious which is mostly responsible for what you believe and the conscious which is mostly responsible for what you conceive, will begin rendering the results you desire. Soon, you will be achieving that goal you aspire to.

All of this is much like gardening. You always have to make sure that the soil you use is just right, especially prior to planting a seed. After pouring through mounds of scientific data, these are what seem to be the best mental, emotional, and spiritual exercises for success. Indeed they assist you in the development of a more personalized method of finding and living a life that is in accordance with our true nature.

Make that Change Immediately

You do not have to wait for the right circumstances, nor do you have to depend on luck, to make real transformations in your life today. Mind over matter, right?

Now is the time to make up your mind to do the following so that you can begin to see positive changes in your mindset and life immediately.

➢ Make a clear decision that, this is the way forward for you.

➢ Stop thinking negative thoughts altogether. If you do, then don't be upset. Chalk it up to practice and try again. It may take a while to break an old habit, but do what you can to get negative thoughts out of your mind so that you can replace them with positive ones.

➢ That includes negative self-talk as well. Quit bashing yourself. Not only are you your own worst critic, but at the end of the day you are your own best friend. Begin treating yourself a bit nicer.

➤ Do not continue to dwell on the things that are wrong or missing in your life. Stop worrying about what is not happening to or for you. It does nothing for you, but instead only serves to drain you of your precious energy. Everything happens in perfect universal time, but only when you are ready.

➤ Start living from an attitude of gratitude. Take a moment and consider how lucky you are, to be healthy, alive, loved and amount of abundance that you have in your life right now.

➤ Start giving credit where credit is due. Now is the time for you to take notice of all the good things in your life. Your existence may not be perfect or even ideal, but there is something about you and your life that is worth preserving and sharing. Pay more attention to these things and less attention to what you are lacking.

➤ Ask yourself, "What am I grateful for?" each morning when you wake up and take note of what happens (especially in a journal).

➤ To keep a level head is a virtue. Know that it is alright to have and show emotions, but letting your feelings get the best of you is not conducive with success or happiness.

➤ Constantly reflect on the successes you have already achieved up to this point, even if those achievements are seen by others as small or insignificant. What matters to you does not necessarily need to matter to other people. At the end of each day, you have to count your blessings so you can secure more for the same.

> Before you go to sleep, make it a habit to review all of the things that worked out in your favour for that day. This is how you essentially rewire your higher self—filling it with memories of freedom, opportunity and possibility.

Changing your life is a lot simpler than you might think. As cliché as it sounds, it is possible to live your dreams if you want it bad enough. Transforming your life is as easy as transforming your mindset and habits one day at a time.

CHAPTER THREE

Mind Mechanics and the Technology of Success

Now that you understand what a holistic mindset is, you must also grasp the fundamentals of making that positive change to your life. On top of that, you also have to use all the tools you have gained to begin making that transformation right away. What's next is that you must learn more about the key concepts of the holistic mindset, the technology of success, and the importance of using your whole mind to move in one direction without opposition.

As discussed, the mind is comprised of a consciousness (or awakened mindset) and an subconscious (or sleeping mindset). Although most of our decisions, behaviours, and actions are dictated by just 5% of our minds, it takes 100% of it to get anything done. If your subconscious says that you cannot do something then you most likely won't do it. By the same token, if you simply believe that you can do something but refuse to put any real effort into the endeavor then you most likely won't see much in return. The key is to use the whole mind, and not allow yourself to rely on that bossy 5% of your mind to make things happen.

You should understand by now what the SPAM system is all about. This breakthrough science is based upon the ability to know and replicate behaviour modeling. In other words, it is mind training for those people who are serious about making positive changes to their life for the long run. This structure, with which you conduct your thoughts, behaviours, and actions are what makes up your mental structure. The SPAM system is designed to help you to familiarize yourself with your own mental model, as well as teach you effective ways on how to reprogram your mindset to better suit your personal or professional needs.

The model you ultimately use to structure your behaviour and life is incredibly important to whom you become and the lifestyle you eventually have. It is the foundation for everything you do and will do in the future. So, what exactly is a model?

It is pretty simple to understand what a model is and then afterwards to grasp how it relates to your mental state. Essentially, a model is nothing more than a series of vital building blocks or steps that comprise a structure. Everything in the physical world has a unique structure to it, even your mental awareness. So basically, understanding the building blocks within the model or structure of your personal mindset and grasping the dynamics of the key variables therein will ultimately be what gives you the edge you need to transform your life and reach the pinnacle of success. The tools and techniques explored within this book were developed to help you do just that, and quicker than you may have thought possible.

The Perfect Model

Human beings are different than other species on the planet because we have the ability and the nature to constantly contemplate our own existence. We do this through our consciousness, using the whole mind to reach conclusions about our surroundings. Because of our unique mental capacity, we have an ideal mental model that greatly fosters more happiness and success in our lives. This is what is known as the *Perfect Holistic Model.*

The perfect model for human beings is to exemplify the holistic model. In order to successfully do anything you must adopt a holistic mindset—one that has all of its component parts in perfect harmony and balance. It may seem like a difficult task, but when you consider that the holistic mindset is the natural state of human existence it might then seem a little easier to attain. When all is said and done, maintaining mental balance is ideal, and a holistic mindset is just that.

So, now that you know what a model is you will need to better understand what exactly a *holistic* model is. As part of the natural state of things, the holistic mindset model is comprised of 4 basic parts—each coinciding with its own unique part of the self. Understanding these components is essential to being able to make the most of your unique mindset.

4 Main Components of the Holistic Mindset System

Luckily, the holistic model's main components are pretty simple. As innate parts of every living organism, the holistic model is centered on the most natural state of being. It is simplified to offer the most benefit to those who adopt it with an open mind, a workable plan, and have a willingness to make the appropriate related changes to transform their life.

The four main components (or elements) of the basic holistic model are as follows:

1. **The Physical**: This portion of the holistic model represents your **body**. It is centered on maintenance of your physical health and wellbeing. As a main component of a proper holistic mind, the physical element is as important as any other. If you have not taken proper care of your physical self then the rest of your life become increasingly difficult.

2. **The Mental:** This portion of the holistic model represents your **mind**. It is centered on the filters through which you see the world. Those global and personal programs that have been hardwired into your consciousness actively affect your conscious thought process. The mental aspect of the holistic model is what determines your ability to inspire and/or attract others to you.

3. **The Spiritual:** This portion of the holistic mind represents your **Deeper Mind**, Inner **Spirit** or **Higher Self**. It is centered on formulating and regulating your deeper consciousness—the life forming part of your mind where you keep all of your memories, beliefs, values, thoughts, and experiences. The spiritual aspect of the holistic model is what imprints different things onto your consciousness and ultimately determines how your life turns out.

4. **Pass It On (Societal):** This portion of the holistic mindset represents your **relationships**. It is centered on the importance of your ability to pass on to others on Earth and to those in your personal circle what you have learnt. Through you exhibiting the right behaviour and successes, others will be inspired and attracted to you and want to have what you want. The social aspect of the

holistic mindset model is what determines your personal responsibility to the world you share with other living beings—inspiring their inner spirit (true nature) and helping them to light up from the inside out.

In order for you to successfully understand and live the holistic model you will also need to understand the mechanics of the mind. You have to grasp the concept that you have a conscious and subconscious mind, and that there is a split or inner conflict between the two. This can be a blessing or a curse, and it all depends on how you structure your mental model.

When you become consciously aware of the world around and within you, and when you understand that you can actively control your thoughts to judiciously police the thoughts you have, the world begins to open up for you. Being the manager of what ultimately gets imprinted on your subconscious mind is what will allow you to close the gap between the split and use your whole mind.

Having your mind in a holistic and whole state is essential to everything in life. It is only when the mind is not in an aligned and congruent state that conflict occurs, either internally or externally. In order for you to move in one direction you will have to streamline your way of thinking by adopting holistic mind mechanics. With discipline, concentrated and serious practice, virtually anyone can transform their lives this way.

The Importance of Learning the Tricks of the Holistic Trade

Most people know the quote from Descartes that goes, "*I think therefore I am.*" Although this quote has a lot of truth to it, the whole story would be better summed up by this quote by an unknown philosopher: "*I think therefore I am not. It is only when the mind is silent that I am.*" The importance of learning the tricks of the holistic trade are contained within the self-calming and mentally-stimulating skills you will learn therein.

With practice, you too can learn how to master your thoughts and/or even stop them altogether. This will allow your inner presence to join with your spirit and align itself with your destiny. It is in this holistic mental state that you can more easily communicate with the Universe—with Life itself. It will guide you along the way and show you what to do when those curve balls are thrown. Indeed, right here is where the power of creation most naturally resides in its most potent form.

Your entire life will change when you embrace and operate from a holistic mindset. Using the mechanics of your mind you will be able to recognize and work in collaboration with your own inner presence. In fact, you can build your inner presence by feeding your mind a healthy mental diet of positive thought, and by being mentally vigilant as to what you allow to ultimately become imprinted on your subconscious mind.

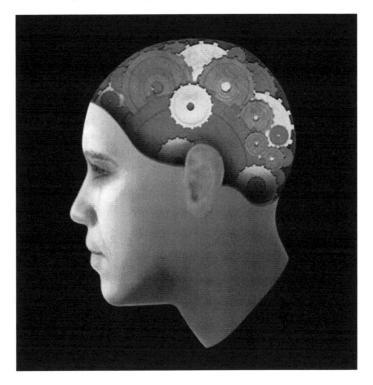

In order for you to make the most of your newfound knowledge regarding the mechanics of the mind, you will need to be careful about what you focus on. In addition, you will need to do whatever you can to develop and maintain a healthy and supportive environment.

Instead of training your mind to expect or blindly accept negative stimuli, you will be setting up a mindset that mostly acknowledges the successes in your life. For this reason, every single achievement you make needs to be immediately and permanently imprinted onto your mind, and then you need to let other people know about it too. This, in and of itself, is the truest form of self-development. You are simply training or developing your deeper mind or self to build success upon success. By sharing and acknowledging your successes with yourself and other people, they too then collectively hold your successes in their minds so that they are stored in the collective subconscious allowing for more of your success to come about, thereby strengthening and growing your inner presence.

It is not difficult to spot a person who has a strong and true presence. Most of the time, other people are inexplicably drawn to those with a strong presence or charisma and as a result he or she is usually able to make some pretty big impressions on the people whom they happen to meet. Since you and you alone are responsible for the impression that you present on other people, it becomes important for you to master your own mind mechanics for the benefit of the bigger picture.

Another thing you need to realize is that you are the creator of everything that ultimately happens to you. Indeed, the results that you are currently getting out your endeavors are of your own doing. You are a complicated mix of emotions, thoughts, beliefs, values, memories, hopes, and abilities. Having the strength and knowledge to customize those things about yourself is what separates the people who are successful from the defeated.

Your life is the feedback in the form of results or successes of how well you understand and use the mind mechanics model and how well you are able to work in partnership with that Life creating part inside of you.

Keep in mind that you are what you eat, and you "eat" more than just food. Remember that your mental nourishment is equally as important. When structuring and maintaining your personal mental mechanisms, do what you can to keep an eye on things like:

- The thoughts you have
- The things you watch
- The words you hear and use
- The internal monologue you have with yourself
- The way you view the world
- The company you keep
- The music you listen to
- The preconceived notions, beliefs and values that you hold about people, places, or things

- The things you fear
- The things you hope for
- The memories you have

These are the factors that will become who you are; they will become your nature, your character, and your life. Having the correct mental diet in all aspects will allow you to walk more confidently along the road to success. It is by the habit of diligently developing a wholly holistic model of thought that you can finally promote more effective mind mechanics.

How the Holistic Model promotes better Mind Mechanics

Remember the mention of the mental autopilot that we all have? This deeper mind aspect is where all of our memories and former lessons, experiences, and hopes are stored. The actions we take and behaviours we exhibit are all drawn from there, even in ways that we cannot always be aware of it. Based on the filters that we have purposefully, accidentally, or unknowingly placed within the mechanics of our mind, we experience life in that way.

In recent years there has been a lot of research conducted on the power of the mind to affect reality. Through a series of studies, it has been identified that success is directly linked to our ability to gain access to our personal mental control centers. In other words, success in any given goal is guaranteed only when the person who has that goal is willing and able to take control of what is imprinted on their consciousness—replacing doubt and negativity with confidence and positivity.

For this advantage to be yours as well, you will need to get the attention of your subconscious mind. Remember the deeper mind is important because it is the 95% of your consciousness that dictates the majority of your thoughts, emotions, beliefs, and actions. By accessing this part of your mind you can thereby imprint or learn whatever you want, virtually reprogramming your mind to render the outcome you desire the most to come about.

Inspiration is the key to unlocking the potential of your deeper mind. Nothing makes your mental capacity open more welcomingly than participating in an activity that you enjoy, or more so by doing something that is in line with your personal or professional objectives. This two-way cooperation between your actions and your thoughts will eventually translate into a more positive and inspired existence, which in turn will allow you to more easily reprogram your mind.

Inspiring your Conscious Mind

Getting your mind fired up and ready to receive new data is not as difficult as you might believe. When your subconscious mind is imprinted with what you want then your autopilot begins to move towards it—filtering information around you to find the most appropriate and worthy opportunities. Inspiring your conscious mind will also inspire your subconscious mind, thereby allowing you to make the changes you want.

You see, the wide world around us has virtually everything we need to achieve our successes. Anyone can become anything, as long as they have the tools and skills to do so. The key is to ensure that you have the correct subconscious filters in place to recognize opportunity when you see it and then, take appropriate and well planned action towards achieving what you want. If you are currently not getting the results and success that you want in your life, then now is the time for you to start applying the mind mechanics model.

Abundance, in all essence of the word, means that there is more than enough to go around in the world; it all starts in the mind. Why should someone else have abundance and not you?

The only difference is down to the fact that the successful person has learnt how to use their mind to effectively create the successful results that they want.

The good news, it is easy and now you too can start to create successful results with the simple understanding of information contained within this book.

The holistic mindset (or model) is what helps the mind to promote this abundant phenomenon. This is mainly because your whole mind is employed, with no opposing thoughts or emotions getting in the way. In essence, a holistic mindset gets the entire consciousness aligned, which allows for a more precise movement and a sharper focus in one single and planned outward direction.

In short, this model turns your mind into a programmed target-seeking missile—aimed at conquering your chosen objective.

By practicing the holistic model on a daily basis, you will start to program your mind for success.

Mind Mechanics: The Key to Success

The fact of the matter is rather simple: your mind is always switched on—working nonstop regardless of what you do or where you go. Regardless of the steps that you take to control any given situation, your mind is going to be filtering through stimuli anyway. It is essentially an operational mechanism of the mind. It is not meant to be self-destructive but rather a simple mode of operation for the mind.

Due to this inevitability, you have to continually make choices on how to respond to the stimuli or events presented to your mind.

Will you be at the mercy of any and all negative programming and conditioned behaviors or will you finally take control of the natural process of thought and manifestation in order to live the life of your dreams?

Will you be the cause of success or failure?

The good news is that it is never too late to redesign what filters are used by your subconscious mind and you can start immediately.

Fortunately, there has already been some breakthrough research performed in this area and more is being discovered about the mechanics of the mind every day.

Over the last three decades there has been enormous breakthroughs made in the field of neuroscience. There have been extensive studies on the biology of the brain and the systems that underlie behavior.

There is no debate that mind mechanics are the key to success, or at least the control of them. With this understanding, you can finally learn how to gain access to your deeper mind, which in essence is your mental control center. Indeed, this is where life happens, based on those things that you implanted onto your subconscious mind.

By simply using a series of success conditioning exercises, you can easily transform yourself. You can reprogram your core values and beliefs so that they are more positive and in line with your true nature. Build your consciousness to become the positive resource it was meant to be. Create something that is internally and externally supportive of your dreams.

It is with this understanding that you can drastically change what ultimately becomes imprinted onto your mind. Use the tools and exercises you have learnt thus far, to customize your mental mechanics— adding and subtracting things at your leisure like a fine-tuned computer. Learn what you want and let go of what you don't, allowing your deeper mind to do the rest by directing and leading your actions based on your conscious requests.

Use your newly imprinted and resourceful beliefs to restructure a value system that is conducive with your goals. All your former learnings and experiences thus far have served a valuable purpose, but if this is not serving your overall objective or it is not in line with your life's vision, then it may be time to let it go. A holistic mindset (or model) is what will allow you to take inventory of your own mind mechanics and make changes where you see fit.

Imagine what you could do with your life if you allow yourself to truly embrace and act from the holistic mindset. The science is right there, proudly boasting humanity's ability to manifest a better world one mind at a time. The power of the mind is a fascinating mystery, but new technology is allowing us to tap into more and more of its potential everyday– and for the benefit of all mankind.

CHAPTER FOUR

The Life Force: Exploring the Law of Reciprocity

It is not every day that the average person takes a moment to stop and really consider why they believe or behave the way they do. For the most part, the majority of people in the modern world today, think that their actions are dictated by their current situations. In a way they are, but the cause for our decisions comes from a much deeper place than that—a spot in our consciousness that most of us are not even aware of. In short, your subconsciously-developed beliefs are what drive you, controlling your life without even giving you a choice in the matter.

It is important that you understand all of this on a primal, fundamental level. If you have a set of beliefs that you are clinging to with claws, wouldn't you like to know where these beliefs came from or how they were formulated? Even if you don't, having a basic understanding of their origins will help you take control of your own life in ways you might not have ever dreamt possible.

The fundamental constructs of the Law of Reciprocity affect us all, regardless of who we are or how hard we try to hide from the unavoidable. If your core beliefs drive you to behave or choose in a certain way, but are created under false pretenses, you may end up making the wrong decisions. At the end of the day those decisions determine your fate, and the Law of Reciprocity is unforgiving to those who have acted in ways that are opposite of their goals or true nature.

The Echoes of Life and Belief

Life is an echo—a variable hall of mirrors which is a reflection of your thinking. In reality you are the echo, a mirror that reflects back on life, your interpretation of what you think on a daily basis whilst you are alive. Life itself is a serendipitous, complementary, and symbiotic journey, whereby you are the captain of the ship. The ship—better known as reciprocity—carries you along the tumultuous waters safely and securely, as long as you have constructed a robust vessel. This vessel is your mind.

Understanding ways to develop your inner self will allow you to not only increase your conscious awareness, but it will also foster a greater ability for you to transform your core beliefs. This may ultimately set up a more rewarding system of reciprocity for you, despite the inevitable hardships of life.

Have you ever heard the saying, "What comes around goes around?" Well, there is a lot of truth to that statement. Although it may seem like it at times, you are not living in a bubble. Your core beliefs may make sense to you, but they may be unfamiliar or even strange to others. What matters most is not who is right and who is wrong here. The thing that should concern you instead, is how you are going to use your belief systems and your personal reciprocity to make the world a better place for everyone involved—even those who don't necessarily see the world in the same way as you do. Whatever you give out is what will be reflected back and in essence what you will receive. Some of us may go through our lives choosing to shut off or failing to acknowledge other people around us with the exception of our families and close knit set of friends. However, in reality we are all one and the same. Irrespective of our cultural, religious background or even skin colour, we are all driven by the same primal needs, have the same biological functions and we each have a mind.

Expecting or needing others to see the world through your eyes can come in handy in certain social situations which makes it a valuable part of the human psyche. However, the behaviour itself can get in the way of your goal when you are trying to perfect your mindset, find your true self, connect with others, or walk the path to your destiny. In actuality, the act of imposing your beliefs on someone else is not only rude but downright immature and counterproductive.

Think about it: what you send out into the world eventually comes right back to knock on your door—often in ways that are unclear to us until after the fact. If you are able to discover the secrets to your subconscious mindset composition, then you might still be able to unlock your true potential (and make a few friends while you're at it). The world is filled with a multitude of belief systems—all stemming from a variety of worthy sources. Your beliefs are just as real as anyone else's, but by the same token, they should not be the fuel for the fires of judgment and can all be easily changed and perfected to serve you.

In order for you to understand the impact that global belief systems have on you and the rest of the world, we first need to define what a belief is. A belief, by definition, is pretty simple:

"Belief: An acceptance of a statement that is of or about the existence of something; a firmly held opinion or conviction."
—Miriam Webster Dictionary, 2014

There are many different synonyms to the word "belief" as well, and knowing them will help you to determine whether or not what you think is based on fact or imposed opinion. On top of that, knowing the related definitions will assist you in being more perceptive during basic conversations as well. In short, this knowledge will allow you to keep your chosen personal convictions intact while still being open and accepting of others' points-of-view.

Some of the most common substitutes for the word "belief" are as follows:

- Opinion
- View
- Conviction
- Judgment
- Idea
- Impression
- Theory
- Notion

- Principle
- Ethic
- Tenet
- Faith
- Dogma
- Creed
- Credo
- Doctrine

The list of synonyms goes on and on, but these are some of the most common terms used in place of the word "belief." Regardless of which word you use or hear, you will need to grasp and respect their origins in order to get a better understanding of how they impact your own true nature. Then, you have to use your understanding to foster within your own consciousness a greater reverence for the true nature of others who share this reality with you.

When it all boils down, beliefs are nothing more than generalisations we make—rules we place on ourselves based on what we have experienced in life or been told to be true. The fact of the matter is that, you need to set up your own beliefs, even sometimes in spite of what your experiences have taught you.

You will know when you hit the target, but do you know how? It will be because you believe you have hit it and for no other reason. That is why belief is such a powerful thing. It can hinder you and help you out at the same time, depending on how you use it.

The whole world is filled with different people who all have their own personal beliefs. Even more than that, we live on a planet with groups of individuals who share a set of common beliefs with one another. These are what are known as "belief systems" and are usually referred to as religions, life paths, or dogmas. Global belief systems are just as delicate and powerful as those personal convictions mentioned previously.

Understanding Global Belief Systems

As human beings we all need something to cling to—something that helps us make sense of the world that we live in. As a result of human evolution, we as a species have decided that our learning curve is cut short when we observe or mimic the beliefs and habits of those around us. We long to establish meaning in our lives, and we want nothing else than to fit in somewhere. This fundamental need is essentially the main reason why global belief systems, or worldviews, are created in the first place—to shed light on the unexplained portions of existence.

Global belief systems, though intrusive and often illogical, are pretty vital to modern life. These are usually formed after generations of gathered knowledge has been accumulated and passed down, either by word-of-mouth or by written histories, and they are most commonly used as a basis for moral behavior. A comprehensive global belief is sometimes referred to as a "worldview." What you call it is not as important as what you understand about it. Luckily, a global belief system, or worldview, is a pretty simple concept to grasp because you live in it every day.

Fundamentally, a global belief system is nothing more than a collective cognitive orientation, a thought process that is shared by a large group of people, or more simply  a society of individuals that encompasses a body of attained or formulated knowledge. The unique point of view held by this "society" is what is sometimes known as a philosophy or creed. A typical worldview usually even includes those existential and/or normative postulates, themes, emotions, morals, and values that have puzzled people since the dawn of time. These variables are often what give global belief systems their mystique and allure.

This world-wide perception usually has nothing to do with the individual, other than the fact that using his or her acceptance to sustain the doctrines thereof is essential. The general framework of ideas, dogmas, and opinions are what make up that which we most commonly accept to be the reality of our existence. We use global belief systems as a culture to watch and interpret what the world throws at us. We need beliefs to make sense of the life we live in, just as we need a road map when we travel to distant lands. However, just as we need to make sure that our road maps are leading us to our ideal destination, then we need to ensure that our belief systems are steering us to our ideal destiny in line with our life's vision.

While certain people hold the view that individuals are solely responsible for the development and maintenance of worldviews and/or global belief systems; others seem to think that these belief systems are an inescapable factor of community living. In fact, modern research suggests that we do this (formulate belief systems) as a collective on some mysterious and as yet undiscovered subconscious level.

For example, we all believe the things we do based on where we were born, how we were raised, and other unique deciding factors. However, if we were to live under different circumstances then our worldview would surely be vastly different. We would literally have to "put ourselves in someone else's shoes" in order to understand where they are coming from. This is just not that easy for some people, though for others it comes quite naturally. The key is to understand how and why any given global belief (or personal belief for that matter) has been accepted and established.

According to many modern experts who study global belief systems and other important sociological patterns, a person's worldview is usually based upon attaining the following:

- An acceptance of some understandable explanation of the ways of the world

- An answer for the direction of the future—"Where am I going?"

- An answer to ethical questions and inquiries about values—"What should I be doing?"

- A theory of action, or some sort of methodology for our lives—"How should I be acting?"

- A belief of what is true and what is false, usually to a certain measurable degree—"What is real to me?"

- An etiology of your own system, or in other words how it came to be—"What were my building blocks?"

It is the need for the answers to these fundamental questions that ultimately drives people to develop unique or shared belief systems. In addition, the primal human need to live or interact with other people, and/or to reinforce their beliefs through recognition, eventually spawns global belief systems to develop naturally over time. These things together comprise the subconscious mindset that most of us take for granted.

As mentioned, your personal beliefs are most notably based upon the global belief systems into which you were born. These rules or regulation are meant to dictate what happens to you, as long as those rules are met in accordance to the agreed upon doctrines thereof. Still, sometimes we like to (and should) make our own rules. The rules we make for ourselves also need to make sense for our own personal bottom line, whilst still working for the bigger picture as well.

The Rules we Make for Ourselves

Every one of us has a set of rules that we live by—obligations and limitations that we use to monitor our behaviors, decisions, values, and beliefs. If you stop and think about it, you could probably come up with quite a few of your own rules pretty quickly. In some instances, you might even find that you share your rules with close friends, family, and co-workers. At other times, not so much. Both instances should be expected and are completely acceptable ways in which to live.

By the same token, you may encounter a circumstance where you and another person share the same value on something, but not the same rule about how it should be handled. This imbalance between belief and value is usually one of the major causes of conflict, and it has been the case since the dawn on human existence. The development of global belief systems has stood to complicate matters in many ways, especially in modern times, in that it has more or less given mankind yet another reason to quarrel with themselves and others.

Still, rules have to exist in order for society to function in an orderly fashion and for all of us to co-exist more or less in harmony with each other. It is this symbiotic relationship that comprises life itself. Remember that your beliefs and rules are important but that they can also be transformed based on need and desire.

For example, you can hold the belief that you will only be happy and successful once you've attained a large sum of money and be miserable while you slowly climb the ladder of success. Or, you can make a rule that you will choose to be happy on your journey of success despite your financial circumstances, and live a life full of joy and contentment instead. Remember though, achieving success does not necessarily mean that you will have no more motivation to create any new beliefs, rules, or goals. Life is always evolving, you are always growing, and success can always be achieved on several different levels.

As long as you are intently committed to growing as a person and as a productive member of society then you can set up nearly any goal and see it come to fruition. Having something to aspire to can keep the spark alive inside you, making you feel challenged even after you feel like a success. The motivation to achieve even more will be yours, but only if you are willing to transform yourself from the inside out, including but not limited to a consideration of your commitment to the personal global belief systems you hold so dear.

Finding the Keys to Understanding and Transforming your Core Beliefs

Your core beliefs are based on a mixture of all sorts of things that make you a one-of-a-kind person. To put it as simply, our beliefs are just generalizations of what we think has to happen in order for things to be true for us. In other words, what we believe can be very subjective depending on your basic foremost learnings or experiences, which were most likely determined by early social and environmental factors.

As discussed earlier, most of us have values and beliefs that we did not design ourselves—dogmas and rules that are outdated to say the least. Unfortunately, some of these beliefs are taking mankind in the wrong direction—one about which we have no clue. This is one of the main reasons why a lot of these global belief systems are not serving us very well, and it is a clear example of how quickly people cling to something in an attempt to remove confusion and make sense of their lives.

Fortunately, we have the ability to make choices and as mankind, do not have to live with this fact without some solace or hope. We can change our beliefs quite easily and the changes and benefits can be very rapid. Adopting or installing new beliefs that actually serve our true nature can often be as easy as changing your mind about dinner. Okay so it is not always that simple, but it can be a lot easier for you if you open your mind and heart to the possibility that you just might know what's good for you more so than some foreign and outdated collective consciousness.

The fact of the matter is simple: any outcome, emotional state, or core value that you want to attain can be accessed by your subconscious in an instant. All it takes is you making the decision that you want to make the change and then simply rewire your neuro-pathways using repetition so that it is properly installed. If you make up your mind to reprogram your deeper consciousness, then nobody can stop you. All of the emotions that you could ever have are nothing but physiological reactions that you continually create in your mind. Essentially all that is required for you to recreate your core beliefs is having the ability to:

1. Identifying your old beliefs
2. Defining and choosing new resourceful beliefs that support you that you want to replace the old beliefs.
3. Installing the new beliefs using the technique of success conditioning by focusing your attention in the right way and using repetition.

Most of your frustrations about the lack of success in your life comes from the fact that you have some lousy beliefs and values. These "rules" were most likely created by someone else and then they were ingrained into your subconscious mind through the years to become your reality. To date, you have been controlled by values and beliefs that were ultimately stored in your autopilot without your own choosing and you have been experiencing life based on these subconscious filters that were not yours by choice or design.

As you now know, whatever is stored in the top drawer of memories and beliefs etc. of your subconscious mind (the 95%) is what will be led out to form your life. So, now is the time to design your own subconscious filters.

Remember that what you believe you keep, life follows thought and form follows function. Although it is true that you cannot always control the circumstance of your environment, you can control how you react to that environment. To this end, who you surround yourself with becomes of paramount importance. With this understanding, I hope that you are now beginning to realize that the things you think, say, and do on a daily basis really count towards the quality and success of your life.

Understanding and Defining your Core Beliefs

Your core beliefs are pretty easy to identify. Most people have the same basic premises through which they structure their primary values. These generalizations are our fundamental understandings that we have made about our lives, the people, places, and things in it. Because of this, the majority of people describe their core beliefs in one of these familiar forms:

> ➤ *Life is...*
> ➤ *People are...*
> ➤ *I am...*
> ➤ *That/This is...*

So after considering these different forms, you will then need to ask yourself a few questions:

- What kinds of beliefs do I have about who I am as a person?

- How do I see myself and the world around me?

- Do the beliefs I hold dictate how much of my skill or potential that I use on a daily basis?

- Do the beliefs I hold empower me?

- Are my beliefs, values, and morals resourceful?

- Do they affect the quality of my life?

- Do they have an impact on the amount of success I do or do not have?

- Do they have an effect on my willpower or willingness to try new things?

- Do I have similar beliefs to others or are mine out of the ordinary?

Remember that what you hold to be true in life is also what you keep in your mind and habit. Never forget that whether you believe something is true or believe something is not, you are right. Your beliefs are the driving force that opens up your inner power and universal possibility. That is why limiting beliefs ultimately shut you down and immediately create a chain reaction that limits you in ways that you couldn't imagine.

Having certain beliefs is essential for survival, but others can be downright counterproductive. We all have them, those generalised beliefs that we have adopted throughout years of living. Believing that people are wholly honest or innately dishonest is a prime example. Thinking that people are naturally givers or that they are unapologetic takers is another instance where our beliefs get in the way.

If you can relate to any of those examples you are not alone. However, you do need to take responsibility in considering how your beliefs make a difference in the way you treat those around you, especially those whom you judge before they ever even speak. Some beliefs can be potentially dangerous, as has been proved in the many wars that have been waged over fundamental values, instead of people practicing tolerance. The most notable examples of this can be found in the ethnic cleansings during WWII and the genocide of Jews across Europe, or the covert affairs portrayed against the innocent Tutsi people of Rwanda.

Have you ever stopped to consider the scope of modern global belief systems? What about those beliefs and/or religions where the devoted followers happen to believe strongly that their point-of-view is the only right one? We are all too familiar with those worldviews where the devotees are even willing to kill or die for the beliefs held within that particular paradigm. These conflicts are usually placed under the category of "Holy Wars" or crusades in favour of one global belief system and against another.

We see this in our history as a species as far back as it has been recorded. We still have a long way to go in terms of resolving our differences which all come down to conflicting beliefs and values. In recent years, we have seen lots of trouble in the Middle East with Muslim and Islamic extremists. Before that, we could cite the troubles with the Catholics in Northern Ireland or the Christian Crusades and the "Holy Wars" that took place in centuries past.

As you can see global beliefs and values (and the programs and mindsets therein) can be very distractive and on the whole are not world-changing. When you are born, you naturally have some learning to do which is dictated by your given cultural background, and you will eventually operate from the values and beliefs you develop from that. However, life is not found strictly within those lessons or rites of passage.

To know your own deeper mind—the one that drives your true nature—you will have to understand the influence of those programs and/or lessons that make up your particular mindset. It is only when you begin to grasp the fundamentals of this that you will be able to see how these special mindsets ultimately have dictated how you have lived your life thus far. On top of that, you will also discover just how much your own deeper mind affects the global belief system in which you participate. This breakthrough in realization is when your whole life changes.

It is our beliefs that determine which questions about life that we find ourselves willing to ask at any given time. The inquiries we make of ourselves then determine what we focus on throughout our daily lives. This eventually changes how we feel about ourselves and the world around us. So, the beliefs we have are what dictate what rules we place on our own existence. It is as simple as that!

Rules are the big *"If* and *Then"* of life. If you are told one thing about a group of people or a global belief system then you will most likely act in accordance to how that information makes you feel, even if that information is mostly false. We all have rules for everything in our lives. Remember, rules are how we make sense of the world around us. The key is to not let these rules get in the way of truly experiencing all that Life has to offer you.

For example: *"If you make a lot of money then you will feel more successful."*

As a modern person you probably make a judgment call on people immediately regarding how you think they should act or be. This happens sometimes without you even meeting the other person. We all do it. We have a preconception or expectation of how the other person should be or behave.

More often than not, you might discover that some of your "rules" are too complicated for your own good.

Some may even be in conflict with what you are trying to do, tying your consciousness in proverbial knots. The net result is usually nothing short of overwhelming—frustration, discouragement, and hopelessness to put it mildly.

To be successful at the business of living a fulfilled life, you need to create your own rules and make them as simple as possible so that you can win at the game of life. Doing this does not mean that you have to set your standards low. It does mean, however, that you will make it a lot easier on yourself, especially when it comes to achieving your goals and getting along with other people.

True Self-Development: The Model for Life

To create an ideal model for your own life you will need to foster true self-development in everything you do. The most fundamental law of nature is that things either grow or they die. Since life is always evolving. It becomes essential that the person also learns to evolve mentally, physically, emotionally, and spiritually by using their entire mind in order for them to thrive. Relying solely on just 5% of your mind will no longer suffice in today's world. It is only when you use your whole mind that you build an inner presence about yourself and naturally become one with life itself.

What is Self-Development?

Self-development is a pretty simple concept—one that should be learned by each and every person walking the planet today. Indeed, it is an investment in yourself and the future of the entire world. It is having an invaluable ability to learn and grow by using your whole mind. It is learning how your mind works and how to apply and use that understanding to increase your inner presence, then working in collaboration with your inner spirit (or life force, subconscious mind, fate, etc.) to create a wondrous life.

By learning the keys to self-development you are ultimately able to take full responsibility for your own life. This is what will give you the power to understand and use the subconscious mind. Operating from this holistic mindset often means making a big difference in the world around you, and it starts with yourself and ends with those with whom you come in contact. Becoming truly invested in your own self-development process is what will eventually make you a better person. You work in partnership with your inner spirit, that pure, loving, intelligent, abundant energy, whose purpose is to look after you and make the best better.

True Intelligence of Self-Development

To possess true wisdom and intelligence you need to learn how to work *with* life and not *against* it.

Contrary to popular belief (there's that word again), life really only exists within the subconscious mind. Every single message or request made via your deep thoughts has to inevitably pass through the rules and regulations of life itself. This is when it eventually responds to you, but you first have to build up your own inner presence so that you can be seen and heard, so-to-speak. By developing this conscious awareness you allow life to recognize and communicate with you.

> *"You've got to stand for something or you will fall for anything."*
> *—Aaron Tippin*

Surely you do not want to be a puppet and at the mercy of your own subconscious mind do you?

Remember that whatever gets put onto your subconscious is considered real. As a result, life will play along in the form of manifesting good, bad, success, failure, happiness, and despair based on whatever is stored in your top drawer virtual filling cabinet of your subconscious mind.

Most of us at one time or other have experienced periods of pure personal magic, where everything we do or touch seems to fall into place effortlessly. Some people call this effortless flow or intuition. But imagine if you had true intelligence about the mind mechanics. It could eventually be turned into the virtual technology of success, at least on a personal level. In reality, there is an actual structure (or model) for all of this. Within your subconscious mind is where the magic lies. By understanding the mind mechanics model, you begin to learn how to access this true intelligence and learn how to work in collaboration with that intelligence to bring about what you want to experience in your life.

Combining the Holistic Mindset with the Life Force

Now that you completely understand what a holistic mindset is, and you grasp why it is so important to your personal bottom line, you can begin learning how to combine your new conscious awareness model with the life force. Life is an echo, as we covered earlier in the book. What you send out eventually comes back to you, albeit not always in a way that you recognize immediately. However, if you spend a lot of your time dwelling on negative beliefs then you will most likely find yourself living in tumultuous circumstances one way or another.

It all comes down to this: what you get through to your greater mind will eventually become your reality. Essentially, what you believe is what you keep. What is held inside your deeper mind is what you will use to process your reality. This will dictate your actions and inactions and eventually your fate. If you truly understand this at the core of your being (not just intellectually) you can use it to become successful at the business of living and everything that comes with it.

The holistic approach and using a holistic mindset to get through life means that you keep an open mind and do your very best to see everything in a new light. By drawing a line in the proverbial sands of your mind, you then give yourself a new way of perceiving things. A person who understands and lives from a holistic mindset will see themselves and the people around them as vital parts of the fabric of life.

This newfound mindset will create a perspective that will allow you to view global belief systems in a new light. You will not be using those preordained global mindsets to see other people as separate from yourself, in some sort of fragmented reality. Those who fully adopt a holistic mindset will look at the capacity and power that is life itself, and they will recognize the creative possibilities therein. In short, adoption of a holistic mindset allows you to use your energy to become the director of your own life.

You see, "Life", "Higher Self" or "Spirit" has a direction and movement that is all its own. It's main aim is to evolve, hence it has a vested interest in the evolution of mankind, because it can only evolve through the virtual conscious awakening and evolution of mankind. This is why a holistic mindset needs to be added to our day-to-day lives. It actually creates cohesion between our spiritual and physical bodies while fostering a greater chance of personal success in the meantime. A holistic person seeks a greater understanding of life and is mostly invested in self-development, focused on growing their inner presence, and improved awareness instead of concentrating on the trials, tribulations, conflicts, and differences that exist as a natural part of existence.

Granting yourself access to the greater (subconscious) mind and then being aware that you are using it consciously awakens the *"thinker"* within you. Self-development involves harnessing that part of life within each and every one of us—the part that brings about our successes into being. With this unique and fundamental understanding, you then make yourself consciously aware that we are all a part of the magic of life, and you know it in your soul to be true.

The Mindful Mental Diet

I hope you agree that you are conscious because you are alive—because you live and breathe and take in experiences. To that end, I hope that you then recognize that life is also within every living thing. At this point, you should be able to consciously awaken your mind in order to look at the bigger picture. Remember that you reap what you sow and you can only see in others what exists within yourself. With this key understanding, you realize that the life force inside of you is also in other people, therefore we are all one and the same. Because you know this, you will begin to treat that part of you with greater respect and reverence. Your life force or spirit has a vested interest in you, because when you start to self-develop, it will in turn evolve. So, your life force will work in partnership with you to give you what you want. The more you share this other people and help them self-develop, the faster this magic will work for you.

Also, remember that from one small candle you can light many. However, you first have to learn how to be that light. Knowing your own true nature is synonymous with living your true destiny. What you give—to yourself and to others—is what the world will give back to you. Like a huge mirror that starts from within the depths of your mind, life reflects only what we show it. So, if you believe something without a doubt, then magic will surely happen naturally as a result.

Most of us know how to dream or wish for what we want in life. However, by really understanding the creative processes of our greater (subconscious) mind we only need to know what we want, we do not have to dream about it. This is basically because we virtually imprint our wishes onto our greater mind and the rest happens naturally.

Life will reflect all of this in the form of results as feedback. The more you understand the complex relationship between your coherent thoughts and your subconscious mind, the more successful you will become at getting the results that you want. It is when you understand this that the good parts of life begin to manifest in your life. Luckily, the holistic mindset is applicable to any person, business, or country and can even eventually become the natural way of the world.

The job of your greater mind is to lead those deep thoughts that are imprinted onto your subconscious mind and eventually give you a fabulous life that allows you to make the best even better. This is essentially why it is so important for you to always be very careful about your mental diet. You need to stand guard at the doorway of your subconscious mind, police your thoughts and remembering that life always follows thought, only allow the good thoughts to be filtered through onto your deeper mind.

Start to see the potential in the 'Higher Self' or 'Life', and learn to see it in a different way. This all begins with you being the light that illuminates the lives of other people in a holistic way. The more you are able to work in partnership with your 'Higher Self' to direct the deeper mind, the more successful you will be at the business of living. This is what will draw other people to you, because people love to be inspired. Start to share the model with other people, and show them how they too can use it to design and create successes in their own lives. Draw out and grow the light from within yourself and other people by thinking and saying only good things to yourself and others.

Combining the life force with your holistic mindset is what will bring you joy, fulfillment, and success. It will allow you to connect with other people in ways you never dreamed possible, while fostering a greater ability to manifest your own destiny. That in essence, is the life force in action.

CHAPTER FIVE

Mastering your Thoughts and Emotions

There may be a lot of things in life that are downright impossible for you to control, manage, or fix, but your own thoughts are not one of them. Inside you lies the power to completely transform who you are—from your own personal beliefs and values to the filters you may or may not use when communicating with other people. Mastering your thoughts and emotions is possible if you give yourself credit where credit is due and if you start practicing right away.

Whether we know it or not, one of the biggest setbacks we experience in life is ourselves. In other words, we are constantly in our own way. No, this does not mean that we have some sort of out of body experience wherein we can physically get in the way of our own path. What it does mean is something a lot simpler. Getting in our own way generally means allowing our innermost thoughts and emotions—both conscious and subconscious—ultimately to dictate how we see the world and what we do with it.

Luckily, there are enough people who understand this simple concept and thus they are able to foster appropriate change among those who do not. Learning from other people is always a great way to save yourself some time and effort, but there are a lot more sources of knowledge than just learning vicariously through others. In fact, there is a lot that you can and should learn from yourself as well.

Taking the time to think about your past, present and future is an important part of knowing what you want out of life and getting it. Considering all of these essential things in any manner not only gives plenty of perspective and motivation, but it also gives you the clarity of mind that you need to transform your way of thinking as well as your life. Indeed, the landscape of your existence depends so heavily on your mindset that it scarcely can change without your thoughts and emotions changing first. In other words, your mind takes the lead and leads out the life you want out into the universe, so it only makes sense for you to begin your transformation right at home—with yourself.

Now all of this might seem kind of unfair to you, especially if you have been trying as hard as you possibly can to make changes and develop a vision of your ideal life. The fact that any change starts from within in a key concept for you to understand and accept before you can hope to see any kind of favourable results. It may be something difficult for you to grasp, but it is essential to achieving any kind of success on any kind of level—personally and professionally, mentally and emotionally, physically and spiritually. In short, you are and will always be what you think you are and what you think you become. Therefore, the responsibility and first step on your journey of transformation starts with you.

Your future depends pretty heavily on two major considerations: what you have learnt from the past combined with what you are doing with it in the present. If you want to ever make anything of yourself, if you want to transform your life, or if you crave to live a life that is conducive with your dreams, then you are going to eventually have to start learning ways to rewire your mental control center. Right now, you may be thinking that, the circumstances of your life may be currently holding you back, but when you change the way you think, circumstances become immaterial because new thinking gives you access to new areas of your mind, allowing you to see new possibilities, which enable you to soar to new and amazing heights in the process.

You may have ingrained beliefs and values that may or may not be serving you. Now is the time for you to start picking them apart and finding out whether or not you are carrying around dead mental or emotional weight. Learning how to get rid of that negative programming of your past is an essential part of making the most of your present and future. You will not be able to see the light at the end of the tunnel if you are constantly wearing the blinders of your past. You cannot move forward in your vehicle of life if you are navigating via the rear view mirror.

You might hear a lot of information about the value of living your life in the moment, and for the most part that is some pretty good advice. At the same time, there is a good chance that you will also hear about the importance of learning from your past. In addition to all of that, you can pretty much bet that you will also be receiving advice about how essential it is for you to be constantly preparing for the future. Although all of this is quite true, there is more to the story. The secret to it all is to find a customized way to do all three at the same time.

This task is not as difficult as you might be thinking. The best way to get it done is to separate the past, the present, and the future into three groups and then consider them on their own. Eventually, you will need to step back and take a good, long look at the big picture with all things taken into account. For now though, simply taking a little bit of time to consider the past, present and future simultaneously is enough to get the ball rolling on your personal transformation.

Knowing the value of your own personal knowledge and having the ability and courage to muster that wisdom in a way that will propel you towards your ideal life is the mark of a truly happy and successful person— someone who is whole and confident while being free enough to accept new learnings as well as the challenges. That priceless personal data of stored memories that lies deep within you is not meant to hold you back, but instead, it is designed to teach you invaluable lessons about yourself and the world around you. The trick is not to wallow and make the past your burden, but to learn from it and use it wisely to your advantage.

Being able to rewire your personal mental control center is practically the only way to attain or maintain anything that you accomplish in life. As luck would have it, good things and bad things can happen to us all. However, when we have worked hard to develop a strong personal resolve then, we are more easily able to surmount any and all of the challenges of life. The only way that this can be done is if we know ourselves from the inside out and better than anyone else on Earth.

This personal excavation might take some time, and you can be sure that it will take plenty of strength and effort, but if you can pull it off then you will be one step closer to achieving any goal that you set out to conquer. In fact, knowing everything about yourself from your past, your present, and your potential future is the best weapon you can have against anything that tries to defeat you. Your enemies and challengers in the form of negative thoughts will most definitely be using what you don't know against you, and if knowledge is power then you will want to be personally powerful in the face of adversity by being completely familiar with what makes you tick.

The most successful people in the world are those who have embraced the facts of their past; they are happy people who use what they know to live life to the fullest while simultaneously staying in the moment, and they are just smart enough to also plan for the inevitabilities of the future while allowing new ideas to flood into their conscious and subconscious mind. Although this might seem like a difficult task, it is actually the natural state of things and it is actually very

simple. You only require to identify the ingrained beliefs and values that no longer serve you and replace them with the ones that do, so that you can benefit from this holistic mindset and new way of being.

Some of your current values, beliefs, and filters are not what you think they are. Although they may seem rather natural to you, the source of them is often extremely tainted by personal opinions and prejudice—often from other people. What once made sense for you in the past may not make sense to you anymore in the present. And the truth is some of these values and beliefs may not be of your own choosing anyway. Being brave enough to let go of such things and make way for new beliefs and values is the only way you will ever truly live life to the fullest.

In order for you to make the most of your life, to transform your whole life in a remarkable way, you will need to walk through the door of opportunity and embrace the changes that you are able to make, just like a new dawn. A fulfilling and holistic life is waiting for you on the other side. Letting go of your beliefs that no longer serve you or the world is the only way that you will ever be able to achieve this feat.

A lot of the times, what we believe about ourselves or the world we live in is something that is so ingrained in our subconscious that we do not even know where those beliefs came from. We do not know why we believe them and we do not know how to let them go. This can be a slippery slope for someone who is unwilling to keep things in check, and it can be equally damaging to anyone who refuses to take a closer look at it. Unfortunately, because the average person is unaware of how their mind works, they fall victim to their own subconscious trap, and they get so deeply wrapped up in it all that, they fail to see the bigger picture. Restructuring how you see yourself and the world by first rewiring what is in your subconscious, allows you to set it up, so that you can win at the game of life. Because you now understand the mechanics of the mind, you know the importance of having an subconscious mind that is fit for purpose. One with the right fertile soil for all of your good thoughts or programs to land on and be nurtured. Armed with this level of understanding makes traveling through this tumultuous and challenging life a whole lot easier and a lot more rewarding.

Changing your Past: Learning how to get rid of Negative Programming

There is no doubt that your past is what made you into who you are today. At no point should you look back on the events of your past and regret anything, even those things that were not exactly positive. Everything that ever happened to you or around you did so for a very good reason. It is your job in this lifetime to recognize the lessons that were given to you and use them to improve your life and the life of others.

Using what you have been taught is the key to succeeding at anything, and is indeed the secret to maintaining anything that you achieve. Letting your past dictate negative emotions and thoughts in your present or wreck your ideals of the future is self-defeating to say the least. This book is designed to help you efficiently sift through your past so that you can use it constructively in your present and future.

Learning how to get rid of negative programming from your past is as simple as you make it. For some people, it can be a rather difficult task because they are unable to think about certain things or unable to let go of others. Changing your perspective and looking at the events of your past from an objective perspective is one of the best ways to get this task done with minimal effort.

Though you cannot really physically go back and change something that is fixed in the past, you can however, change the meaning of any given memory or experience by simply changing the associated emotional intensity attached to that memory, thus giving it less impact. By doing this, you simply "change" the past, by changing how you think about it. The events of your past will always be the same but how you may feel about them will change drastically, by just making this simple adjustment and modifying the emotional weight associated with that event.

For example: By simply changing something that used to make you feel furious to something that is slightly irritating gives you a completely different, lighter less emotional response doesn't it?

You do not want to simply disregard your past, no matter how painful it may be. Taking the time to really consider what happened is a valuable task that is worthy of your consideration. However, take care not to dwell and get yourself immersed in the past memories / experiences. Approach this exercise as a casual observer. Indeed, your past has value but you have to be willing to see your past for what it was, just the past. You can visit as a casual observer to gather valuable lessons but it is not a place to live. Living in the past is not the way to get things done.

The science of the *"**The Inspired Mindset**"* and its highly effective techniques are designed to help you reach a holistic and open-minded understanding of yourself and the world you live in, from the beginning of your existence all the way up until the end of your time here. In fact, if you use it just right you will be able to reap the benefits of this technology and mind transformation process even throughout eternity, as it is made to serve the mind as well as the spirit.

How do you ever expect to live a fulfilling life if you are always stuck on the things that happened to you in the past? Yes, those things have shaped you into who you are but you do not have to stay that way you know. Things happen for us, not to us—and when you finally realize that fact you will be able to let go of the negative programing of the past while still benefitting from the lessons that you were meant to learn from them. Really, the only way you will ever be able to do this is if you begin considering your past with an open, honest, and objective eye.

Some of the things in your past that ultimately shaped who you are can be hidden deep within the reaches of your subconscious. In fact, there are many people who question their own reasons for believing certain things once they consider the things that took place in their past. The thing is, we begin developing beliefs and personal perspectives long before we are aware of it, and often our perception of reality is shifted into something negative before we ever have a chance to do anything about it. When you take back control of your life by learning how to rewire your mental control center however, you actually circumnavigate this avoidable problem and you can finally say that you have your desired life within reach.

Changing the Perspective on your Past

The way you see your past is completely up to you. The facts will always remain the same, but the way you interpret those facts is the key. Like a detective who is gathering clues to solve a hot case, you should be using your past as a link to your true nature instead of as a weight that holds you down.

Changing the perspective on your past is a lot like swapping the lens on a camera. You already have the vision and the equipment, and now all you have to do is put things together in a new way. The vision of your dreams is completely within your control whether you realize it or not, and getting what you really want is just a matter of learning all the appropriate lessons from your past and then using what you know to create a picture-perfect life.

In other words, you have to stop giving credit to the people who hurt or betrayed you in the past. It was their job to teach you certain lessons, not to make you bitter and regretful. By holding onto the past in this way, you will never be able to change anything, and you will ultimately end up completely discouraged as a result.

Changing the way you think about your past while you are still young enough to do something about it is important, but hopefully with age comes wisdom. The older you get, the more you get experienced at the business of living and the more aware you will become of the true facts of living. Ultimately, this is what will lead you to see the world from a different perspective. However, if you learn this lesson early on in your life span so much the better, because you can just get on and focus on living a fulfilled life in all variety of positive ways.

However, it is never too late to change the way the picture appears, and getting it done is usually a lot easier and quicker if you just decide to do it instead of pussy-footing around about it. Whether you would like to see your past in Technicolor or just pick out the important parts is up to you. However, you should keep in mind that your personal camera of the past should always remain focused on as many details as possible, especially when you are trying to change the way your past affects you. Forgetting or refusing to consider certain things from your past can also be a recipe for disaster. Remember that the key is to enter this endeavour as a casual observer rather than a fully-fledged participant.

Some of the best things in life come from our past—reunions, trips down memory lane, hindsight with its 20/20 vision, and so on. Not everything that we will be considering from the days gone by will be negative. However, it is important for you to think about the lessons learned and opinions or prejudices formed during these seemingly positive times so that you can be sure you don't have any hidden negative programming that you will have to deal with later.

If you really stop to think about it, most people form a basic opinion about a given situation based on a rather small sampling of examples. For instance, we typically learn the way the world works by observing the dynamics of our own families or close circle of friends. Although this does serve as a pretty logical basis for our future beliefs, it is rather silly to stop there if you want to be honest with yourself.

Not saying that your friends and family are wrong about everything, but if you were to decide on anything else in life with such a limited amount of information you would surely be called foolish. Your friends and family and the events you all shared in the past may have their rightful place in your heart, mind, and on Memory Lane, but you really need to stop and think about whether or not they are serving you today (or if they have the potential to serve you in the future). If you feel as though they don't or won't, you have to be brave enough to let them go.

This negative programming can sometimes be so deeply ingrained in us that we find it nearly impossible to let it go. It just makes sense, and thinking about life working in any other way would create more questions than answers. This is a pretty common issue for many people, so you should not feel like you are alone. What's more, you should not feel like you are completely wrong either.

Many of us think that getting rid of that negative programming that is jammed into our mind and soul is not easy. When your past has intertwined so intricately into your present, it can be quite difficult to see your future in any clear sense. Take as much time as you need to consider the events of your past and how or why they shaped you into who you are today. This process can be healing in helping your conscious mind come to acceptance and begin to align with your subconscious mind.

Be patient, eventually, you will get the alignment that that you are looking for even if you have to ask yourself a few new questions along the way. After all, that's what the journey of self-discovery and the development of a holistic mindset is all about. Removing negative programming from your conscious and subconscious mind is just a matter of shining a new light on it, illuminated in your spirit through a clearer and much higher quality lens.

Living in the Moment

Ok, so enough about the past. There is a reason why life moves on. Living in the present, wholly in the moment, is the best way to be. In fact, many scholars insist that this is the only way to true bliss or spiritual enlightenment.

It is true that living in the moment is a truly great idea, just look around at your surroundings right now. What about your current situation could be changed or improved upon if you simply acted right this instant? Could you make your mark on the world? You bet you could.

"Life is what happens while we are busy making grand plans for it."

—*Unknown*

Even in the smallest of ways, your life is being lived out one moment at a time and we are swimming through it in a pool of what is known as "the now." This liquid "now" is tangible and can be manipulated at your will. You might not be able to go back and literally change the past and you can't exactly know what the future will hold, but you can live in the moment and take back control of your life.

Being able to embrace what it happening right now without focusing on the past or worrying about the future is the mark of a truly healthy, happy, and well-adjusted person. Don't become confused, however, it is not a skill that is easy to achieve. Most people are wired to consider their past experiences before they do anything else, especially when they are confronted with something new or challenging. Someone who has learnt how to live in the moment has discovered a way to turn off that nagging internal voice of the past and can simply enjoy the experience of being alive.

Rewiring your mental control center in that way is no easy task, so don't feel discouraged. You have to literally stop yourself each time your mind starts to wonder back to the past. If you have taken the appropriate time to consider all the lessons that the past had to offer you, then you should not be too bogged down by questions about it today. If you find that you are, perhaps you should go back and do some more self-reflection until you feel more comfortable in your own skin.

Eventually, you will need to take back control of your own destiny and to stop allowing the events of your past to rule the roost. Your current moment is called the "present" because it is a gift, and to ignore that because you are too focused on the past is like spitting in the very face of your creator. Living in the now, however, is honouring your purpose on this plane while paying homage to the greater cause.

Like any skill, being present and living in the moment takes practice and discipline.

In an earlier chapter we discussed a much simpler method of practicing the art of being present or paying attention using your five senses in the present moment. This can be done with any task that you may be undertaking. Whether you are out for a walk or just simply brushing your teeth.

Practice paying conscious focused attention to your surroundings using your five senses for a given period of time; this will help you in unlocking your mental control center. You may even find that you have insights. New ideas will begin opening up through this process, bringing new possibilities even ones that may have been unrelated to the initial thoughts.

You know better than anyone your own inherent value. You know what you are good at and what you are not, your strengths and shortcomings.

Many of us have a primal fear that living in the moment will mean that we have ignored something important in our past or that we have failed to prepare for the future. Living in the moment is an art form that requires practice and discipline. Start by simply paying conscious focused attention to your surroundings using your five senses for a given period of time for any task that you are undertaking and soon you will be creating your own masterpiece.

Finding the Perfect Balance

Achieving the perfect balance between learning from your past and living in the moment is difficult but it is not impossible. Honestly, it is easier than you might think but a lot of people find it so hard because they just cannot get out of their own way. Your story can be different, but you have to come at it with an open mind.

Mastering how to live in the moment or being present is key to achieving a holistic mindset. Living in the present requires you to be fully aware of your surroundings and your effect on it. By being in the present you find that you have insights and new ideas through this process. A world of new possibilities will begin opening up to you.

Though this will be unfamiliar territory for you, you will begin experiencing a lot of new and exciting things. In short, living in the now will allow you to open your eyes to new opportunities while helping you meet wonderful and inspiring people.

By now you should have already started to define your own beliefs, despite the confines of global belief systems, familial experiences, and so on. Where does the present fit into that equation? Are there changes that need to be made or are you finally content? The only way you will ever be able to make transformations in your life and develop a new and healthier mind about it all, is if you start practicing to live in the moment and answer those questions for yourself.

Finding the perfect balance between using what you have learnt from the past and living fearlessly in the moment is like learning to walk a tight rope. It takes a bunch of practice, requires discipline and you really have to be willing to learn. You need to be able to see the value in it or you will never take it seriously. A tight rope walker has a passion for his journey, and so should you.

Don't let your past have too much say on what happens to you today, and try not to worry so much about the future because it will get here soon enough anyway. The thing is, if you have a good plan for the future in place and you have also taken the appropriate amount of time to consider what the past has taught you, then, staying fully present in the moment becomes easier with practice.

Don't believe everything you think

You need to finally realize that the best way to live is in the moment, and the only way you can do that is if you also understand that you are not just a collection of your thoughts. Life is what unfolds right before our eyes, but we often let it slip away because we are busy worrying about the future or reminiscing about the past. Squandering precious moments of your life because you are doing such things is not living.

In fact, this habit of majoring on minor things is one of the main causes for mental fragmentations, disintegration, and incoherence. In this modern age of so many distractions, it can be pretty difficult to live fully in the moment. To overcome this, you have to constantly be working on something constructive while simultaneously concentrating on the practice of attaining and maintaining a sense of stillness and calm. Instead of worrying about work while you are at home and home while you are at work, you need to appreciate the now and stop letting your thoughts control you.

There is a reason why mindful meditation techniques work so well at improving people's overall moods, fostering better communications, and increasing a person's sense of wellbeing. The best way for you to ever achieve that sense of balance that constantly eludes you is to pause your mind from thinking of the past and the future, and allow yourself to purposefully embrace what's happening right now. In other words you have to do things without always concentrating on doing them and just focus on simply *being* instead.

No matter how busy you are you should still be able to stop every now and then to take the time to take a breather, assess what's important right now, look at the big picture and how you perceive the present moment. Maintaining a state of intentionally active and open attention to the present moment will be what ultimately allows you to live a more mindful life. Knowing that you are not just some collection of your thoughts and experiences is important; though that is a good way to simplify who you are it is not all there is to the story.

To understand this, you really have to make an effort to live in the present moment. And if you live in the moment then you will be able to recognize all of that while you also transform yourself into a casual observer. In short, you will turn yourself around and go from being an open-minded and willing participating in life instead of someone who is constantly judging what you see or assigning negative connotations to it.

Eventually you will find the balance that makes the most sense for your life. This will involve you being one with your thoughts and emotions—neither grasping them too tightly nor rejecting them fully—in order to awaken yourself to new experiences. It is only when you can finally cultivate that nonjudgmental awareness for the now that you will start to fully reap the benefits.

The Benefits of Living in the Moment

There are a lot of good reasons why living in the moment and existing with a mindfulness about you is wholly beneficial to your health. Meditation classes, literature, groups, and even seminars are popping up all over the place—each of them teaching the techniques and benefits of mindfulness (living in the now). In fact, many of today's doctors actually recommend it to some of their patients.

According to studies, living in the moment can do a lot for a person's wellbeing. It can reduce stress significantly and put a stop to anxiety. It can give your immune system the boost it needs to fight of infectious diseases and it can even reduce pain in the body. In some more fantastic cases, maintaining a mindful existence was even shown to help some patients cope with and heal from the effects of cancer or other chronic ailments.

You can usually tell who is living in the moment and who is not, just by simply looking at them, regardless of whatever physical handicap they may have. As a whole, mindful people are happier and more energetic people who have a certain passion or exuberance for life. In addition, those who are able to live in the moment are also more able to muster empathy for their fellow man, since they are typically more accepting of their own shortcomings.

When you anchor your awareness in the now instead of in the past or the future you are more easily able to take control of your surroundings. You don't feel as scattered or impulsive and it takes a long time for any sort of depression to take hold of your psyche. On top of that, you will be able to pay closer attention to the things that are happening right before your eyes, instead of being constantly distracted by your own out-of-control thoughts.

There is no doubt that fully living in the moment and being more mindful requires you to accept a pretty obvious paradox. It really only just takes some trust in yourself and in your creator.

There are many ways to achieve mindfulness and finally live in the moment. Ironically, it is only when you let go of what you truly want that you will ever actually get it. In much the same way that the athlete plays terrifically well in the zone until someone asks how they do what they do and they find it hard to articulate it. Through discipline and daily practice, you too will find your zone and get into it.

6 Simple Methods for Learning how to Live in the Moment

If you ask around you will most likely come across a lot of advice on how to let go and just live in the moment. Although one thing might work for a specific person, there is not a single surefire way to get it done. When it all boils down to it, learning how to live in the moment is a skill that must be customized to fit your personal and/or professional needs.

Here are 6 incredibly simple tips on learning how to live your life more mindfully and wholly in the moment:

1. **UNSELFCONSCIOUSNES**—Improve your performance in anything by not thinking about it. Just do it.

2. **SAVOURING**—Stop worrying about the what-ifs of the future by simply concentrating on the details of the present moment. Know your place.

3. **BREATHE**—To make the most of any situation you should always try to inhabit the present as much as possible. Be there.

4. **FLOW**—If you want to make the most of your precious time you have to go against what you believe and just lose track of it. Let go.

5. **ENGAGE**—Know and accept that you do not know everything but be willing to learn. Stay connected with your inner presence, and trust it to guide you, and you just follow the next step.

6. **ACCEPTANCE**—The best way to get rid of something that is bothering you is to move towards it rather than away from it. Embrace your fears.

Rewiring your hard drive that is your mental control center in this way will no doubt require you to invest some time, discipline and practice. Your past has its place and so does your future, but you cannot live in the moment or enjoy its gifts if you do not at least give it a try.

Remember that finding balance in it all is very important. Your life is always evolving and it always will be, even when you don't really notice it. In order for you to be as prepared as possible for what's ahead you will have to stop worrying about it so much, trust in that higher power to guide you and look after you. Results and feedback are everything. Though it may not make sense right now, it will once you start to put all of this into practice.

Changing the Future: Setting Goals and Developing your Life Vision

We all want the best for ourselves and for our loved ones. If you are brave enough to be honest with yourself then, you will be able to easily admit that something may be missing in your life. Whether you have explored the catacombs of the past or have mastered the art of living in the moment, you still need something to look forward to in order to be happy and fulfilled in life. For this to ever happen, you have to start setting some realistic goals for the future by developing some sort of vision for your ideal life.

Most people generally work really hard for the things they want or need. And although some people tend to feel adrift in the world despite these things, everyone ultimately wants to feel as though their life is worthwhile. The only way for you to ever achieve this sense of fulfillment and accomplishment for yourself is if you start thinking about what you would want your future to look like.

Setting goals is extremely important, especially if you want to transform your mind and life on your own terms. Sure, you have conquered your innermost thoughts and emotions, but what good is that if you do not have some tools to do something with your newfound skills and abilities? Life is a seriously complicated journey—a series of hard-earned lessons and blessing that often come in disguise. Being able to make a successful existence out of that requires you to get yourself prepared.

The main reason why a lot of people feel as though they have no idea what they want for the future is simply because they have not sat down to really think about it in any serious or honest sense. People are so busy these days that they often neglect themselves in order to provide for the bigger picture. Although there is quite a lot of honour in this act of selflessness, the "machine" is essentially only as strong as its weakest link.

Would you set out on some kind of journey or adventure without first plotting your course or at least having a few key directions? Would you go anywhere without having your necessary accoutrements such as, money, communication devices, and so on? Probably not. The only way you can ever expect to make it through life in any cohesive or potentially successful manner is if you start setting some formal goals for yourself right now.

The Power of Goal Processing

Having the ability to set some appropriate and realistic goals is like having a super power. It seriously allows you to streamline your life's wishes and it actually guides you step-by-step through your reality until you reach your objective. This powerful process that is smart goal setting and vision planning is what separates the successful from their not-so-affluent counterparts.

Goals are what help you to visualize what you want out of life. They are typically used for motivational purposes due to the fact that some sort of personal will power must be exhibited to turn those goals into something other than ideas on paper. In other words, your goals are only as good as you are—even if you took a lot of time to think about them. You can eventually turn your vision of the future into a reality, but you have to be willing to plan and work for it.

The actual process of setting realistic goals for yourself is not as difficult as you might be thinking, so give yourself some credit. Remember that some of your negative programming may be telling you that you can't do one thing or another, but you never will know until you give it a try. By really knowing precisely what you want to accomplish or achieve, you can then figure out where you should be concentrating your efforts. This is what will increase your success rate at whatever you do and ultimately help you to develop a more confident sense of self.

The power of setting goals by using your vision of the future is what will lead you to where you want to be. On top of that, this sensible preparation will help you to spot negativity and distractions from a mile away. No longer will you be so easily turned from your ideal existence. Instead of going astray you will have the power to stay on the task at hand until you achieve what you set out to achieve.

The Importance of Setting Good Goals

If you stop and take a look around, you will most certainly notice that every single successful or happy person in the world has set some kind of goal(s) for themselves. Good goal setting is important for people from all walks of life—from politicians, stay-at-home-moms, and students, to scientists, philosophers, and artists. It is essentially what allows these people to maintain their momentum and continue serving their community and family in the best way possible.

Setting good goals will allow you to see things in the short-term as well as the long-term. It will also help you to focus your innate and learned knowledge constructively. When you are able to construct appropriately realistic objectives for yourself then you are also immediately able to explore the following important considerations:

- Time constraints
- Personal handicaps and taste
- Outside variables
- Resources
- Unexpected emergencies
- Natural disasters

Failing to plan is about the same thing as planning to fail. Having some kind of plan for the future—one that is in line with your ideal vision of the perfect life—only ensures that you will live out your dreams. If you want to make the most of your time on this planet while honouring your creator you are going to need to know the importance of setting good goals.

When you set out to set some clearly defined goals for the future you thereby give yourself an advantage in life. It is important that you always have the ability to see the fruits of your labour, and that is exactly what happens when you outline some sharp objectives for yourself. You will be able to literally measure your accomplishments and notice when you have made progress. This will eventually translate into an increase in your self-esteem and an improved sense of overall wellbeing.

Life without goals might ultimately end up seeming like an endless grind—some pointless endeavor that goes nowhere. Indeed, you are here for a reason and setting goals is what helps you to realize what that reason is. Developing a vision for your future gives you hope, which is arguably the most important thing in a complicated and difficult life.

Setting Realistic and Powerful Personal Goals

 Here are the keys to your future. However, you cannot drive until you have insured your life with some appropriate goals. Doing this simply takes a little time and patience on your part, combined, of course, with a willingness to make something of your life.

When you have the keys to the future resting in your hands, you want to be sure you are prepared for the responsibility. You can set some good goals that ensure your success and you can accomplish this task rather easily actually. Every single person will have to find their own method that works the best, but as a general rule most folks tend to have great success by following these 3 easy steps:

1. **Consider the Big Picture**—try to think about everything you want to do with your life without considering the obstacles and improbabilities. Be sure to identify your short-term as well as your long-term objectives. Double check that both are complementary to one another.

2. **Break it All Down**—do what you can to deconstruct each of your objectives as much as possible so that you can create cohesive steps towards to the final goal. Chunking things down in this manner helps you to create smaller targets which will ultimately allow you more success at reaching your ideal outcome.

3. **Start your Engines**—use the keys of your step-by-step process to begin working towards your goals with a driving sense of inspiration and organisation. Track and monitor the feedback and results to ensure that you are progressing in the right direction. Utilise your plans to stay on task and continually strive to improve and adjust your processes along the way as required.

If you can follow those three simple steps throughout your goal achievement process you will definitely see some major success along the way. There are a lot of things to consider when you are creating a list of short-term and long-term goals, so be sure to take your time. The future will get here no matter whether you are watching for it or not, so just slow down and start thinking about how you want it to look when it arrives.

Your future is going to be a product of what you have learnt from your past and what you do in the moment. To structure any kind of workable plan around those things you will have to stop and think about some factors that might contribute to the coming years. Now is the time for you to embrace the future by pulling your ideas and dreams into reach and creating some kind of broad plan of action.

You may have your own list of considerations, but for the most part the majority of people think about the following when constructing any kind of plan:

- Finances
- Education
- Family
- Personal Tastes and Artistry
- Ideal Profession or Position in Life
- Mindset
- Trinity: Physical, Mental, Spiritual
- Pleasure and Pain
- Social Perception

THE INSPIRED MINDSET | 141

- Public Service

Take a little time to think about these things and then move through the 3 easy steps that are required for you to start your "good goal engine." The more you achieve the more you will want to work; the more you work the more you will understand and respect the power and importance of setting goals for the future.

Try to feed your lessons back into the process of creating and updating your objectives. This is what will allow you to learn from your mistakes and ultimately develop a better plan for the next time. Keep in mind that your goals will probably change a little bit as natural part of living life. Remain open-minded about this and do not let it get you discouraged. We can never know what the future might hold, but we can learn how to adjust ourselves and our dreams to fit into it.

Using Goals to Master your Thoughts and Emotions

Developing some workable goals for yourself can help you to get a handle on your innermost thoughts and emotions, which will thereby allow you to transform your mind in new and improved ways. Those who have a mastery of their own mindsets are the ones who enjoy the most benefit out of living life. To count yourself among the people who know how to control their thoughts and feelings, you most certainly will

For Information & Inspired Mindset Trainings Visit: www.TheInspiredMindset.com

need to set up some goals and use them to your advantage.

Goals and personal objectives have a way of making life seem a little bit easier. Without a keen sense of what you want and what you should be expecting, unpleasant surprises tend to pop up out of nowhere and leave you feeling defeated. On top of that, a lack of goals can make you feel unconfident over time and can actually force you to develop new thought processes and beliefs that are negative and counterproductive.

From this day forward you need to give yourself permission to forgive the past, live in the moment, and plan for the future. Set some goals up for yourself and keep your dreams in the forefront of your mind. Transform your own mindset once and for all and align it with your ideal life. Take back control of your life by turning these art forms into a lifestyle.

Using goals to help control and master your thoughts and emotions is not difficult. In fact, it just sort of happens out of the innate characteristics of the habit itself. Goal setting is about the same as promising yourself that you can succeed while also saying that you are worthy of the work. Until you can embrace the value of good goal setting you will always suffer from low self-esteem, the effects of unpleasant surprises, and often much, much worse.

Remember that it is important for you to never give up on your dreams, and to keep in mind that sometimes this endeavor means that you will need to ask for some help. If you are finding it particularly hard to set reasonable goals then humble yourself and request the assistance of someone who is good at it. After all, the best way to accomplish anything is to emulate someone who is already a success.

Goals are designed to help you streamline and connect your past with your present and your future. Whatever help you may or may not get, be sure that it is from a well-meaning and knowledgeable source. Remember that not everyone is out to help you, but not everyone is out to hurt you either. Let go of that negative programing of the past and use what you know in the moment to prepare accordingly for the future.

CHAPTER SIX

Training your Mind for Successful Living

We are each one of us responsible for the control of our own minds. What goes into it and what comes out of it are ultimately our decisions, and so aligning our thoughts with our life's visions is important in creating a successful life and it is within our grasp. The human mind is a remarkable piece of perfect engineering machine and though science is still exploring the depths of it we do know that self-programming is a real possibility.

It begins with you having unconditional love for yourself. Although some people might believe that the sheer notion of wanting to change thought processes or improve one's standing in life is the opposite of unconditional self-love. However, this is the absolute wrong way to think. Indeed, it will ultimately prevent you from living a successful life. The responsibility starts with you. Ultimately, you are in control of your own destiny.

In reality, the true key to successful living is to constantly strive to improve your life and the lives of others through conscientious decision making. First and foremost, however, you have to love yourself and be willing to forgive your mistakes and shortcomings. Training your mind to let these inevitable obstacles roll off your back while continually reaching for your goals is the secret to a fulfilled life.

When you hold yourself to a high esteem, you are more willing to accept the things in life that you cannot control while being brave enough to change the things that you can. In addition, knowing yourself well and understanding your own unique tendencies will lead you to better respect your true nature and will thereby assist you in living out your real dreams. If you add self-discipline to the mix, you give yourself the ability to customize your life by training your mind to seek out the best possible scenarios. In short, respecting, knowing, and consciously controlling the thoughts that you are having moment to moment are the things that will lead you to the life you have always wanted.

"Self-reverence, self-knowledge, self-control; these alone lead one to sovereign power."
—Alfred Lord Tennyson

For centuries, scholars from all over the world have lectured on the power of training one's mind to love and respect itself while actively seeking out a controlled sensibility. Using what you know to propel yourself towards successful living is one thing, but the power that is behind this knowledge is going to eventually require some concentrated control. The only way you will be able to do this is if you train your mind—that is to say, create an entirely new way of thinking.

Learning the skills that are required for this is very simple to grasp. You need to ensure that your own thoughts and emotions do not get the best of you before you even get started, because this can eventually lead you to lose your momentum altogether. When the smoke clears, you need to take control of your mind and emotions before they take control of you.

Having the right mindset and training your mind so that it is aligned to your life's vision is just as important to the process of successful living as is deciding your path, planning your moves, forgiving your past, and defining your true nature. It is an essential task that, when neglected, can have some pretty dire consequences. A disciplined and well-trained mind that is well-equipped to survive and thrive in today's fast paced and highly competitive world is what is required.

What does it mean to "Train your Mind?"

In order for you to understand what it truly means to train your mind you need to realize why it is such a fundamental part of everyday life. In modern society today, a lot of people feel as though they are subject to seriously abstract and seemingly interrelated issues. This has a lot to do with the fact that we are all subject to the human condition. Despite what you may imagine, your problems are not unique or dissimilar to other people. We all have the same problems though they often come painted in different frames. Training your mind requires you to grasp this concept so that you can stop thinking that the world is out to get you or nobody can honesty understand your problems. Ultimately, we all want a better life free from worry, war or suffering. A world of abundance for ourselves and others.

It is not always possible for the average person to deal with certain conflicting or controversial social and environmental problems either. Some people actually turn on themselves, seeking out various forms of punishment as confirmation of their ill-fated feelings. To cope with living in such conditions usually requires an extremely fit mind, which is why you need to learn how to train yours. Today's world is challenging and confusing for everybody, but a well-trained mind can be controlled to move through those challenges turning those challenges into opportunities.

Training your mind is a simple concept to grasp. It basically just means that you teach yourself how to adapt according to certain situations throughout life. However, you need the tools and an understanding of how your mind works to be able to do this successfully. Since things are ever-changing, it is essential for a successful person to gain this priceless skill. In fact, many experts are now saying that cross-training one's own mind in this way might someday be just as popular as mainstream physical training.

Effective mind mechanics training requires you to go beyond what you think you know about yourself and the world around you. You have to approach each and every situation with a sort of structured and untethered mental capacity, giving yourself the ability to perceive and achieve amazing feats in your everyday life. In essence, training your mind for successful living means first understanding the mechanics of how your mind works, consciously managing your thoughts and emotions and working in partnership with your deeper mind to make your dreams into reality.

"Don't think outside the box. Think as though there is no box."

—Unknown

We train our minds all the time without even knowing it. That is essentially why we have so many thoughts, emotions, and memories that need to be erased, rewritten, or reconsidered. As we go through our lives we train our minds to perceive the world in a certain way based on what memories or experiences are stored in our deeper mind. When we don't reach our dreams it becomes obvious that this has a lot to do with the way we approached the opportunities we were given.

Whenever we do something that involves variety or choice we actually stimulate our mind, waking it up in the process and forcing it to ask, "What is there to learn from this situation?" Because life is a nonstop series of changes, challenges, and chances it only makes sense that we should train our minds to receive these circumstances as opportunities rather than obstacles.

Mind mechanics training is different than simple mind stimulation. It requires discipline but at the end of the day it is essentially what increases a person's capacity for new and innovative thought and understanding. The philosophy of the *'The Inspired Mindset'* is the fundamental key to changing your life for the better, and it is centerd on creating new thought processes that are conducive with your dreams. So, learning how to train your mind is the first step towards achieving complete mental transformations and sustainable successful living.

How does Mind Training Work?

When you learn how to do something new you train your mind to perform the appropriate steps associated with that action or series of actions. For example, if you teach yourself how to play a musical instrument you essentially learn how to retrieve a number of mental and physical skills from the depths of your well-trained mind. To successfully pull this task off, you will need to train your attention span, your memory capacity, and your motor skills to name just a few. Well, just about everything else in life is set up the exact same way. Just like everything else in nature, the mind works in a structured orderly manner.

Mind training works because new ways of thinking and consciousness is awakened. This new way of thinking creates new synapses in your brain which allow you to perform new skills, whether that skill be playing said musical instrument or transforming your way of thinking. In order for the task to be a success, you have to be willing to practice it for an extended period of time. Just like physical exercise, the mind muscle grows with continued disciplined training. By simply doing a bit each day, will gradually stack up creating fertile mental soil from which you will flourish. Nothing worth doing in life is ever accomplished overnight, unless you get really lucky.

When you actively train your mind to do something that is important or meaningful, your pleasure centers are actually getting activated within you. Your extremely happy and fit mind will then enjoy a stronger cognitive ability, which will ultimately translate into you getting more out of life. If you want to experience successful living, you will need to start training your mind to recognize and accept all that comes along with it.

It is important to note that proper mind mechanics training really only works under specific conditions. You cannot hope to successfully train your mind or transform your way of thinking if you keep doing what you have always done. A lot of people wonder about, which conditions make mind training work the most, because once the process starts it is difficult to stop (mostly because it feels so balanced and natural).

As a result of this curiosity, studies are being conducted around the world which are looking into what it takes to make mind mechanics training more effective. Maximizing the likelihood that specific mind mechanics training techniques will translate well into everyday life is an essential part of getting the most out of your efforts. When you consistently and regularly train your mind with discipline you will be able to enjoy the benefits thereof tenfold. This is very easy to track, measure that monitor as to whether or not the mind mechanics training you are doing is actually working.

The results and frequency of successes that you are getting are your ultimate feedback.

There are a few other important things that you should consider about your mind mechanics training exercise in order to ensure that it is the best option available. You should be especially careful about what you train your mind to do, and so having some guidelines might help you to avoid training your mind to do or think things that will be counterproductive. Based on the most recent research about mental transformations and maximizing the effects thereof, good mind mechanics training should consist of the following:

1. Manage your Thoughts

Watch the thoughts that you are having from moment to moment. Notice the language you use when you talk to yourself or other people. Do you focus on moving towards a solution in the face of challenges? Do you focus on asking yourself empowering questions to get to solutions? Are you continually reinforcing resourceful beliefs and values that support you?

2. Life's Vision

You say and do good things for yourself and other people and act from that mindset. Share the holistic mindset model with other people, so that they too can self-develop and learn how to create their own success and inspire other people.

3. Success Conditioning

Wax lyrical about all your successes to yourself and others. Run a mental movie of all your successes however small. This is a way of growing your inner presence by ensuring that the soil of your subconscious mind is filled with the right mental fertile soil onto which good thoughts can land and be nurtured.

If you really want to prevent your own cognitive decline while improving your chances of living a successfully fulfilling life, then you will need to discover practical and effective ways to train your mind to do exactly that. Remember that not all mind training is created equally, so be careful about what you teach yourself. Successful living starts with you taking back control of your thoughts and emotions through proper mental focus and by defining your own ideal existence once your mind is clear.

Defining Successful Living

Now you might be asking yourself how you will know when you have achieved successful living standards. Practicing all of that mind training is great but what good will it do you if you do not know when it has taken effect? To make sure you always know where you stand in this lifetime, be sure you have a clear definition of what successful living means to you.

Each and every person alive today has his or her own idea as to what a successful life looks like. What seems like a successful life to one person might look like a wasted existence to another. Being open-minded about this part of life is important not only to you feeling as though you have accomplished something, but also to you accepting others for who they are. A truly successful life is whatever you say it is, but it is also always one that is integrated nicely into the existing world. Ultimately, one's life is measured by the success of one's ability to share and replicate the holistic model with other people.

Right now is the best time for you to start thinking about all the ways in which you are going to use your mind training. Will you use it to help you get past certain hang-ups and setbacks? Will you train your mind to accept your shortcomings so that you can concentrate on your abilities and strengths? Are you going to train your mind responsibly and be careful about what you learn?

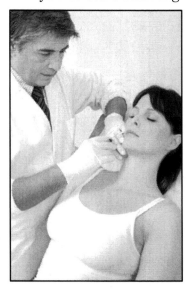

These are things that you will need to think about when you are defining what a successful life means to you, or else your mind training will be more or less an act of vanity—nothing more than cosmetic surgery on the surface of your personality.

Defining successful living is a subjective endeavor—one that is only propelled by your willpower and dedication. Once you have trained your mind to think and feel the way you want it to, you can then move on to identifying what you want out of life. After that, developing a plan on how to get it will seem like a piece of cake. The best place for you to start this incredibly essential process is to use what you learn from this book, specifically *the Sensory Perception Actuality Model (SPAM)* and then incorporate its lessons into your everyday life.

So which of these important life lessons are you going to allow yourself to learn and which ones will not become important to you?

Do you even know how to answer that question? If the answer is no, then that means you need to revisit the mind mechanics model and how that works, then start to identify what you really want out of your life.

This is what will help you to decide which plan of action to take. It will ultimately guide your learning so that you can horn your skills and abilities. In the end, it will also help you in defining a structured plan to the finish line.

Identifying what you want out of your Life: Developing a Workable Plan on how to get there

Getting ready for any amount of personal or professional success means that you first aptly identify what you truly desire out of your own life. This also means turning away from the wants and wishes of other people—those thoughts and beliefs imposed upon you by some outside source—and instead finally listening to yourself.

This transformation from where you are to where you want to be requires a new way of thinking and self-discipline. You first need to make a real decision. It cannot be accomplished in any way, shape, or form without this vital step. In order for you to do any of this, you will first make the decision; this will then propel you in developing a plan of action and steps to take in order for you to reach your overall goal or vision for your life.

Lack of preparation inspires a person to feel less motivated, generally depressed or disheartened, and/or even completely disinterested in their dreams altogether. If you do not want this to be your story, you will have to lay things out clearly for yourself before you move on to the next phase of your life. Indeed, it is having a clear-cut plan that makes a person's dreams seem possible.

There really is no right or wrong way to define your own plan, especially considering every person's final plan will be different. Figuring out what works for you is always the best plan of action. Just focus on the first step, do your homework and due diligence and trust in your higher power to guide you. However, there are some key components that should go into everybody's ultimate plan, or at least the formation of that plan.

In other words, there are certain things that need to be done when structuring a plan for your ideal life. The majority of us are afraid of failure; indeed, this fear of failure is what discourages a lot of people from even getting started.

Remember, preparation reaps its own rewards. A well-thought-out plan can actually be seen as an insurance policy on your motivation and inspiration and as a guarantee on the final favourable outcome.

So now you may be asking yourself what these specific things are that happen to be so fundamental to any well-made life plan. In reality, these "things" are more or less just some important thoughts and/or considerations which you will need to dutifully list before you can take your first step. Doing so will not only help you to focus your attention on your exact ideal but it will also help to streamline your process so you'll know where to go at every turn.

One of the main reasons why some otherwise capable people never really succeed in life is because they actually believe deep down that they can't. Sadly, this is usually not even the truth, or at least there is more to the story. Still, the self-defeating belief is held onto because of all the seemingly insurmountable obstacles that stand in their way.

Another reason is because of unfathomed surprises that seem to pop up out of nowhere. But what happens when we prepare ourselves for these things instead of allowing them to get the best of us?

We become stronger and more resilient people and we also end up giving ourselves a fighting chance against the things in life that are there to "teach us lessons."

The Six Essential Considerations

Below are the six most important things you should be thinking about prior to or while you structure the perfect plan for your life. Don't be afraid to go ahead and add a few considerations of your own to the mix. Just be sure that your additions are in line with your true objective and are not put in place to steer you in the wrong direction.

This part of the process is one which requires you to actually sit down and list some things out in written form. This helps to cohesively bond both hemispheres of the mind and can actually increase effectiveness in the form of improved consciousness, awareness, and confidence. Before you get started you will want to grab a pen and paper or open up a word processing program of some sort so that you can get this done as easily as possible.

Doing this task quickly is not the point. If it takes you a while to list out everything from each of the six essential considerations then so be it. The main objective here is to get clarity so that you know exactly what your plan looks like at the end of this process.

1. List all of things you like and don't like about your life.

There is no wrong answer here. Remember that this list can remain private, so write the truth about whatever comes to mind with no analysis or judgement. Your job here is not to please anybody but to purge your true emotions for your current condition so that you can make the appropriate improvements where they are needed the most.

2. List all of the changes you would make RIGHT NOW if you could.

It may not be possible for you to make any kind of noticeable changes to your life right now, but what if it were possible? Being successful often means thinking successfully before you get there. Write down what you would be doing differently right now if it were within the cards. Don't' be afraid to get down to the nitty-gritty either.

3. List all of the things that you know you can change RIGHT NOW.

There may be a lot of things you cannot do anything about right now no matter how much you wish you could. But still, there are plenty of things that you can take control of right this instant if you only give it a try. What are those things for you? Now is the time to write them all down so that you provide yourself with a motivational roadmap to your dreams.

4. List all of the things that you know can change WITH TIME.

Remember that just because you cannot change things immediately does not mean that they cannot be transformed eventually. Keep in mind that patience is a virtue. Think positively and be realistic about the things that you could possibly change with ample time.

5. List all the reasons why you have extra time to change things in your life.

Everybody is going to have different reasons why they want to make certain changes, and by the same token each person will have their own specific causes for delay. What are yours? Why do you need extra time to achieve certain goals?

6. List all possible solutions to the things that are holding you back.

Only you know why you are being held back or made to wait. So, only you will honestly know the possible solutions to that problem. What can you do to break down a few walls that stand in between you and your ideal life? List them now.

Once you have taken ample time to really think about and list out these six essential considerations you should have a better idea as to where you should go from here. You will know what changes can be made right this instant, which ones you can look forward to later on, and you will keenly know what is standing in your way and what you can do about it all. Indeed, this is one of the most important steps of the life and mind transformation process.

Having things written down and in front of you can really help you to visualize your path. It can streamline your out-of-control and overwhelmed mind. In short, it can train your mind to accept the things it cannot change and to work towards automatically changing the things that it can. Over time, the scope of your life will grow to reflect those transformations.

This is all a part of the personal conditioning process. If you do it long enough and keep up some kind of regular pace, you should be able to enjoy the habit as part of your very own personality. In short, conditioning yourself and your mind in this way will eventually transform itself into who you become as a person and/or professional.

Conditioning Yourself for Success: The Power of Repetition Exploring Neuro-Associative Conditioning Exercises to keep things in Perspective

The only way you can ever hope to condition yourself for success is if you start practicing right away—literally living your life as though you are already a success. You will always have an abundance of hopes and dreams but you have to learn sometime how to keep those things in perspective so that you don't lose your footing along the way. Becoming a success is seldom something that is achieved overnight, and so the majority of accomplished people in this world are those who have had to buckle down and create new mental habits for themselves.

In order for you to gain the skills to achieve this new positively habitual behaviour you will need to familiarize yourself with the fundamentals of success conditioning and the exercises which foster improvements therein. Now, all of this might at first seem a little complicated, but rest assured that is something that we all do naturally every single day. You will just be learning how to rewire or reprogram your subconscious mind so that it works to your greatest benefit.

The true key to mastering and using the benefits of Neuro-Associative Conditioning [7] exercises is that is begets to you the power of repetition. Doing something over and over again only seals the deal, and the more

you do one single action the better you get at it. When you start turning those repetitive actions into positive ones instead of negative ones you are then more easily able to manifest the life you truly desire. In fact, the very act of performing success conditioning tends to improve a person's general outlook on life almost immediately.

Think about it: if you are habitually putting yourself down or thinking about all of the things that stand in your way you are most likely not ever going to recognize the possibilities that lie before you. On the other hand, if you create the right series of daily habits you will begin to turn your life around in small ways, which will eventually turn into very noticeable transformations. Indeed, it all begins in the mind.

What is Neuro-Associative Conditioning?

If you are already keen to the general goings on of the human consciousness (as you should be by now), then understanding the basics of Neuro-Associative Conditioning should be pretty easy for you. Originally developed by Anthony Robbins[5], Neuro-Associative Conditioning, or NAC for short, is a type of programming that the average person can perform on themselves.

The current NAC exercises that one might discover were initially based upon several expert works, all their own system of semantics which generally stated how a person's own experience in life is actually just a representation of reality. With this understanding, it becomes obvious how someone might be able to alter their own perception of reality through certain Neuro-Associative Conditioning exercises.

> *"The map is not the territory."*
> *—Korzybski*

Basically, NAC is just a fancy way of saying that the primary psychological and inner-monologue strategies of a person can be manipulated with the right habits implemented. By shifting these internal representations of "reality" a determined and open-minded person would be able to easily change their habits and eventually their behaviours and beliefs. It is a way of rewiring the neuro pathways of your brain so that they can behave or act differently.

Neuro-Associative Conditioning exercises are designed to help people completely transform their lives from the inside out. The science behind this breakthrough mind training technique is nothing more than a series of simple processes that foster change in the typical human mind. The ability for Neuro-Associative Conditioning to accomplish this is founded on the premise that normal human behaviour is based on two specific factors.

These factors, when looked at more closely, are right on target. They are as follows:

> The basic human need to avoid pain and/or injury.
> The basic human desire to gain pleasure from external sources.

In order for your mind to know how to rightfully sense and positively consolidate these two factors it has to be conditioned just right. That's where Neuro-Associative Conditioning exercises come into play. By training your mind to accept these conditioning exercises as part of your regular behavioural pattern you actually create important "associations" within your nervous system. These associations are what ultimately allow you to make instant and positive decisions that lead you in the direction of your ideal life.

In other words, Neuro-Associative Conditioning helps you to instantly determine the meaning behind any given situation—even the hidden meanings that might have eluded you before. On top of that, this type of mind conditioning helps you to more actively seek out pleasure and avoid pain by directing your behaviour towards the right people, places, things, and ideas. In short, Neuro-Associative Condition exercises are the science of success.

The "NAC" Difference

It is a well-known fact that some conditioning techniques work well for certain people while rendering little to no results in someone else. However, Neuro-Associative Conditioning addresses this problem and is designed to incorporate the most common and effective methods across the board. Neuro-Associative Conditioning can actually be broken down into at least six "master" steps that were developed by experts to foster change within a person's mind and thus within their lives.

These six steps focus on the five basic areas of human psychological intervention, allowing for rapid transformations and little pain getting there. With the right "NAC" exercises a person can change their neuro-associations and make them work to their benefit. In other words, proper success conditioning training can consistently lead a person to discover happiness and pleasure while avoiding pitfalls and pain.

With adequate Neuro-Associative Conditioning you can easily train yourself to always behave and feel in such a way that is supportive to your main objective. This might seem like a rather simple concept, but when you think about how much junk is rattling around in the head of the average person then you can see how retraining the mind to think in such a way can be a complicated matter. Neuro-Associative Conditioning streamlines the human consciousness so that it works in favour of itself instead of the other way around.

When you get right down to it, a person's fate is usually based upon the neuro-associations they possess about pain and pleasure. This typical Success Conditioning model is actually linked to these associations and has a direct effect upon a person's behaviour in certain situations, around specific people, when presented with a new idea, or when dealing with emotion. It is by tailoring your personal neuro-associations that you can feel and behave in a way that is conducive with your ideal lifestyle.

"NAC" exercises are designed to teach people how to perform at their peak. It basically allows you to streamline your thoughts and emotions so that you can stay focused—with your objective in perspective and your eyes on the prize. Being mentally prepared for the long haul while being able to discern the facts of today is the key to success, and it is precisely what makes Success Conditioning so effective for those who wish to transform their lives and reach success.

There are a lot of different types of "NAC" techniques. Each and every method is designed to foster the most change for the practitioner, and they can usually be combined to create an extremely effective tailored technique. Among some of the most popular Neuro-Associative Conditioning exercises are:

- Induction of a trance
- Realignment of personal values
- Establishment of boundaries
- Guided imagery and visualization
- Double dissociative methods for the curing of specific phobias
- Psychological anchoring through visual, auditory, or kinesthetic practices
- Updated vocabulary
- Pattern interruptions and restructuring

Proper Success Conditioning can produce some pretty fantastic results. Although working with a professional coach to carry out Neuro-Associative Conditioning exercises might be the best plan of action, it is possible to accomplish the same outcomes on your own if you do it right. This powerful technique can help alleviate several subconscious and conscious obstacles which will ultimately be the keys to your improved existence, such as:

- *Bad habits*
- *Emotional and/ or Physical trauma*
- *Fears and/or Phobias*
- *Addiction*
- *Depression and/or Anxiety*

- *Weight loss*
- *Self-destructive behaviours*
- *Learning disabilities*
- *Procrastination or motivational problems*

Aside from these important changes, Neuro-Associative Conditioning exercises can help generate a positive outcome for a number of other subconscious issues. By following the six "master" steps of Neuro-Associative Conditioning exercises, you will be able to completely transform your neuro association, which will eventually manifest itself in your waking reality.

The Six Master Steps of Mental and Emotional Change via Neuro-Associative Conditioning exercise

If you have been paying any attention to the lessons given within these pages then you are already well on your way to successful living through adequate Neuro-Associative Conditioning. Essentially, this is a book of Success Conditioning exercises, broken down step-by-step so that you will know exactly what to do.

By now, you should be able to answer the questions asked by the six master steps below. If you feel as though you are not ready to address certain ones then by all means take a step back and think about the ins and outs of it. Be sure to review some of the tools and strategies and methods outlined earlier in this book. That will give you the best chance at success.

Understanding the importance of taking things in small  and easily digestible steps is important. Indeed, this is the best strategy to use to really learn a new skill or technique and will help you in gaining more self confidence and minimize overwhelm. It is the hallmark of a truly happy and successful person. The experts who initially developed today's practical Neuro-Associative Conditioning exercises know the vitality of this, and thus they designed their six master steps to coincide with this innate personal need.

When you are able to master the following Neuro-Associative Conditioning steps you can then consider yourself that much closer to your ideal life:

1. *Know exactly what it is that you want out of your life and relationships.*
2. *Understand what is preventing you from getting the things you want.*

3. *Interrupt your pre-conceived notions and behaviours to remove avoidable obstacles that are part of a self-fulfilling prophecy.*

4. *Choose and begin to use a new pattern of behaviour.*

5. *Condition yourself to accept and practice this new set of behaviours and personality or thought patterns.*

6. *Test out the ramifications of your newly established beliefs and behaviours to see if they work successfully for your objective.*

If you can work to eventually incorporate these six master steps of Neuro-Associative Conditioning exercises into your day-to-day habits you will then have a much better chance at creating an extremely positive automatic response to all stimuli in your life. This is what ultimately spells the difference between success and failure. Earlier, I mentioned that the fastest way to learn is by modeling. Now that you know the steps you need to condition yourself for success, start by choosing 6 or 7 resourceful beliefs that you know will help you to your journey of success.

Here are some examples to get you started:

1. I am successful if I learn from any given situation.

2. Life follows thought, whatever you focus on you get.

3. I am blessed and guided by my inner presence, which will always show me the next step to take.
4. Whatever I ask for, I expect it to be given.
5. Life is a gift to be savoured and enjoyed every moment.
6. Whatever you believe you keep.

I am sure that you can add a lot of more examples of powerful, resourceful beliefs that you've heard or indeed do some research to choose the ones that resonate with you. Install these beliefs to start to create that fertile soil, rich in the correct foundation that your thoughts will land on and be led out by your subconscious mind.

Managing to do all of this is a worthy endeavor even if it is only done for a moment at a time. However, it is usually recommended that you use what you learn from Neuro-Associative Conditioning and its exercises to create a completely new daily routine. When you do this you literally change who you are from the inside out, and if you can use Neuro-Associative Conditioning for positive works then you will wind up transforming yourself for the better.

This might require some discipline, so remember what you've learnt about structuring an effective plan so that you do not let your dreams fall by the wayside when times get tough. Gaining some of that swift of momentum towards your dreams is what you are looking for to eventually achieve your dreams, so letting Neuro-Associative Conditioning help you with that is obviously one of the keys to success. Allowing Neuro-Associative Conditioning to transform your life all the way down to your feelings, habits, and behaviours is something that you will begin to enjoy, and you will come to recognize how self-powered the fundamental laws of human nature really are. You want to get to the stage that your new habits, values and beliefs are so ingrained into your "autopilot" that you naturally act from that.

Just like everything else that has to do with your thoughts, feelings, and behaviours, it all starts right in your mind; and the same can be said about developing and maintaining your motivation. If you learn the proper skills needed to manage your positive mental state acquired through adequate Neuro-Associative Conditioning exercises, you will be able to virtually lock in success no matter what endeavor you pursue.

Maintaining your Conviction: The Importance of Managing your Emotions

You may or may not know this, but your personal conviction to any cause is ultimately what drives you to achieve it or leave it. How you feel about a specific person, place, thing, or idea is the fuel to the fire that causes you to act. If you can transform the way you see these things then you will be able to alter your habits, but if you can alter your habits over a long period of time you will eventually change who you are as a person. This, however, requires lots of discipline and conviction.

Managing your mental state can be tricky, especially in the face of adversity. There are a lot of people who get really far on their personal or professional quests only to be turned off at some point, just short of their destination, only because the road got too bumpy. Indeed, there will come a point when the questions are much easier to find than the answers, but allowing yourself to give up now that you have come this far would be a downright shame.

Despite the inevitable difficulties that are bound to come your way, you must remain steadfast in your conviction to succeed. The importance of developing effective motivational techniques, creating a comprehensive and well-thought-out plan, and accepting what could be learned from various Neuro-Associative Conditioning exercises you should be able to make the promise of success to yourself and keep it, too.

It all starts with you making a decision. Now that you've installed the right set of beliefs and values to support you, consider a set of resourceful emotions or states that you are absolutely committed to live by on a daily basis that will steer you along your journey of success. Here are some examples to get you started:

1. Discipline
2. Gratitude
3. Joy
4. Excitement
5. Curiosity
6. Contribution

You will be tested from time to time by challenges along the way. This is a fact of life. The main difference i.e. the breaking point between the people who let seemingly negative things hold them back and the people who use those inevitabilities of life as opportunities—can be explained quite easily. Successful people have mastered the mechanics of their minds. Their ability to create the habit of maintaining a mindset of positive thoughts, emotions, and behaviours towards life's various circumstances is what ultimately sets them apart. Learning to manage your emotional state is key, since emotions are the fuel that determines what response your subconscious mind leads out.

This is not a difficult endeavor for someone who knows as much as you do by now. You know yourself very well and you have defined what you want out of life. At this point you have structured a plan for your future and you know what you need to do to get it. That in itself should serve as enough motivation to continue working towards your main objective. However, if it does not provide you with the mental strength that you require then you shouldn't be afraid to do what it takes to do in order to keep up the pace.

Understanding just how important it is to maintain this virtually impenetrable mindset might also help you to stay motivated for the cause. Simply grasping the fundamental principles of something is only half the battle. Respecting the fact that these positive and effective mental routines should become a part of your habitual thought and behaviour patterns is what will ultimately give you the power to harness your own internal driving force.

Using your Knowledge as the Power to Succeed

If you happen to have a little trouble maintaining your drive you can always channel your knowledge as a source of power. What you know about the world is unique and it structures what you call reality. You also know just how quickly "reality" can change. Using this innate knowledge to strengthen your resolve will become something of a super power if you do it right.

By this time you most likely understand why planning is so important as well. Did you ever stop to think how horribly your plans might fall apart if you do not maintain your conviction at all times—especially in the face of incredible adversity. Indeed, these hardships are simple tests of your conviction to receive what you are asking the universe for, and so there will always come a point when you have to make a decision to give up or carry on. Go forward with that bit of knowledge, and decide right now that you will stay motivated and focused when your number is called.

"All the world's a stage, and all the men and women merely players. They have their exits and entrances, and one man in his time plays many parts."
—Jaques, As You Like It, William Shakespeare

Remember that you may take your life seriously but you should always try to keep things in perspective along the way. Get out there with your plan in hand and conviction well defined and play the role you have chosen for yourself. All the world may be a stage, but you will have to make it to the show and play your part if you want to find out how the story ends.

CHAPTER SEVEN

Living your Dream: Designing your Lifestyle

Now that you have a good understanding how the mind works and know how to apply some of the breakthrough tools and techniques, let's consolidate what you've learnt into a plan of action.

Lifestyle Mapping

Follow the steps below to create a *Lifestyle Map* for yourself:

The Lifestyle Mapping tool is a visual reference that can help you focus on the areas that you wish to bring back into balance. This simple but powerful tool represents one way of describing the important areas in your life. This vital resource helps you measure the level of Life Satisfaction in all the categories of your life that you feel are the most important to you. It helps you consider each of these areas one by one, assess what is off balance by measuring where you are and where you ideally want to be. In a few simple steps, it helps you identify the gaps so that you can start to map out the journey to creating your ideal Lifestyle.

All these individual steps of the journey add up to make one big adventure we call life!

Below is an example Lifestyle Map for our fictitious friend, Victoria.

As you can see, she has 8 areas that she values as the key drivers that make up her Lifestyle map.

She has then scored them as indicated and marked them on the Lifestyle Map below:

1. Health & Vitality—6
2. Family—6
3. Romantic Relationship—4
4. Finances—5
5. Holidays—4
6. Church work—7
7. 'Me Time'—2
8. Career—6

Then, she has drawn a line to join up the scores in all the areas. This distinct shape, based on her scores, represents her Lifestyle map.

It quickly and clearly shows the areas she needs to address and the steps on the journey she needs to make.

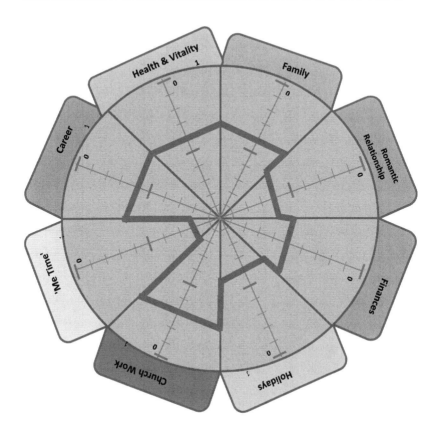

The perfect Lifestyle map is evenly circular in shape, with a score of 10/10 in every category.

But, I am sure you would agree with me, that this would be improbable for most people.

So, let's stick with reality and, as an example, Victoria's map, is very uneven.

The next thing you need to do is to fill out your very own Personal Lifestyle Map.

On the next page is your opportunity to do just that. You will find a blank template to pull out and complete below.

MY OWN PERSONAL LIFESTYLE MAP FOR WHERE I AM NOW

STEP 1

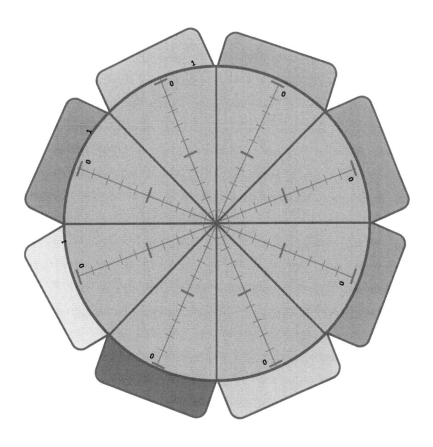

1. Write out the subject areas that you feel are most important and that make up your Lifestyle map. Maximum of 8, as you don't want to make it too unmanageable otherwise you get overwhelmed.

2. Be honest and mark out from a score of 0—10 where you think you are AT THIS MOMENT IN TIME for each of the categories.

3. Using a coloured pen, join up the scores to form your own map.

On the following page are some questions used by Victoria to make her assessment. These will help you come up with your own questions for each of your areas.

These are just some example questions, and I am sure others will come to mind for you as you work through each category of your life that you have identified.

1.Health & Vitality

Q1. Do I have lots of energy to play with my children?

Q2. Do I have aches and pains when I move?

Q3. Do I wake up refreshed and energized?

2. Family

Q1. Do I spend enough quality time with my family?

Q2. Am I a good role model to my children and family members?

Q3. Are my family relationships positive, loving and supportive?

3. Romantic Relationship

Q1. How well do I impact my partner to have a happier life?

Q2. I am happy with my sex life?

Q3. Do I have the level of romance in my life that I want?

4. Finances

Q1. Do I have enough money on a monthly basis?

Q2. Do I have money to spend on the nice things in life?

Q3. Do I have debts that I can't pay?

5. Holidays

Q1. Do I carve out time for myself?

Q2. Do I allow myself holiday time to recharge?

Q3. Do I make time to hang out with my friends?

6. Church work

Q1. Do I do enough for my church?

Q2. Do I like church work?

Q3. Do I add value at my church?

7. **'Me Time'**

Q1. Do I have time for me?

Q2. Do I treat myself to nice things?

Q3. Do I have a good image of myself?

8. **Career**

Q1. I am happy at the level I am at work?

Q2. Is this what I am passionate about doing in my life?

Q3. I am learning and being challenged in my career?

Now you've done it, have a look at your map, take time to reflect on each of the areas and notice how it makes you feel.

STEP 2: HOW DO I CLOSE THE GAP?

The next step is to ask yourself is, what score YOU WOULD LIKE in each area.

1. Using the same **Lifestyle map** that you've already created, mark these scores with a different coloured pen.
2. Join up the scores as before, so that the diagram shows you where the biggest gaps are in your life.

Using the example from before, to close the gaps, Victoria wanted to increase her scores in all the areas that she had defined, to make her Lifestyle Map more uniform.

Here are some example questions that she can ask herself, that I have used with my clients to get some fantastic results. They can help you start to close the gaps such that your life's journey is packed with all kinds of adventure, variety and all manners of good things to help you achieve balance and life satisfaction faster and easily.

1.Health and Vitality

Q1. What are some quick and easy things I can do on nutrition to give me more energy?

Q2. Are there any easy changes that I can make to be healthier?

Q3. Are there any friends that are looking to get into shape that I can join in with?

2. Family

Q1. Are there some activities that we can do together as a family?

Q2. Is there someone I admire as a good role model that I can learn from?

Q3. What are some easy things I can do to support my family members?

3. Romantic Relationship

Q1. What can I do to impact my partner to

have a happier life?

Q2. What am I doing to make my partner feel attracted to me?

Q3. What are some fun & easy things that my partner and I can do together?

4. **Finances**

Q1. What is the sum of money I need on a monthly basis?

Q2. How much money do I need for the nice things in life?

Q3. How much money do I need to pay off my outstanding debts?

5. **Holiday**

Q1. How much holiday time can I schedule?

Q2. What easy things can I do with my friends?

6. **Church work**

Q1. What else can I do for my church?

Q2. What are some things I like about my church work?

Q3. What else can I contribute at my church?

7. **'Me time'**

Q1. How much time do I need just for myself?

Q2. What can I do to treat myself?

Q3. What can I do about my self-image?

8. **Career**

Q1. How can I add value at work?

Q2. Are there quick and easy things I can do to enjoy my work?

Q3. What can I do to grow my career?

STEP 3: OTHER THINGS TO CONSIDER ARE THESE

Asking yourself a bunch of questions is fine because it stimulates the brain...

Drawing and marking some colourful lines no doubt makes a pretty diagram and is nice, but what this boils down to is you taking **ACTION**.

The right **ACTION** has to have the right level of thinking. You have to be getting your mind-set right and your thought process right, which is the foundation of the coaching that I do with my clients.

Having the right mind-set guarantees a strong foundation, which is the key for creating consistent results.

You need to ask yourself:

➤ What resources do you have around you now that will help you take action?

➤ Who can provide you any support and/or guidance?

For example:

➤ **What Professional support do you have that you can call upon to give you**

a quick start and keep your momentum going?

Remember! A strong decision is what gets you started. **But it is habit and the correct mindset that keeps you going.**

- So, do you have someone there in your life to encourage you, hold you to account and cheer you on to keep the momentum going for you?

- Do you want to be part of the new pioneers of mind masters, who are informed, inspired to action, understand and know how to use their minds to create inspirational lives for themselves and other people?

Now is the time for you to get started. Use the Lifestyle Mapping tool outlined above to assess what is most important to you, on the journey to designing and creating your dream lifestyle.

One way to ensure that you are on track is to keep a journal and start to measure and track the results and feedback that you are getting. This will serve as a record that allows you to monitor how well you are progressing on your journey of success and enables you to reassess and make the necessary adjustments along the way.

Paying It Forward: The Life Force in Action

In 2000, Catherine Ryan Hyde's novel *Pay It Forward* was published and adapted into a film of the same name, distributed by Warner Bros. and starring Kevin Spacey, Helen Hunt and Haley Joel Osment. In Ryan Hyde's book and movie, it is described as an obligation to do three good deeds for others in response to a good deed that one receives. Such good deeds should accomplish things that the other person cannot accomplish on their own. In this way, the practice of helping one another can spread geometrically through society, at a ratio of three to one, creating a social movement with an impact of making the world a better place.

Following this, the Pay it Forward Movement and Foundation was founded in the USA helping start a ripple effect of kindness acts around the world. The newly appointed president of the foundation, Charley Johnson, had an idea for encouraging kindness acts by having a Pay it Forward Bracelet that could be worn as a reminder. Since then, over a million Pay it Forward bracelets have been distributed in over 100 countries sparking acts of kindness. Few bracelets remain with their original recipients, however, as they circulate in the spirit of the reciprocal or generalised altruism.

On April 5, 2012, WBRZ-TV, the American Broadcasting Company affiliate for the city of Baton

Rouge, Louisiana, did a story on The Newton Project, an outreach organisation created to demonstrate that regardless of how big the problems of the world may seem, each person can make a difference simply by taking the time to show love, appreciation and kindness to the people around them. It is based on the classic pay-it-forward concept, but demonstrates the impact of each act on the world by tracking each wristband with a unique ID number and quantifying the lives each has touched. The Newton Project's attempt to quantify the benefits of a Pay It Forward type system can be viewed by the general public at their website.

For me, "Paying It Forward" means sharing the "holistic mindset system" and all the breakthrough tools and techniques that you've learnt in this book with other people. You do this by showing and acting with the right behaviors and sharing the successful results that you are having with other people.

This requires you to fully embrace Life's vision. That is, you say and do good things for yourself and other people and act from that mindset. You share the holistic mindset model with other people, so that they too can self-develop and learn how to create their own success and inspire other people and in turn pass it on or "Pay It Forward". This in its true sense is the Life Force in action. You recognise that we are all spiritual beings in a physical body. By helping other people to

THE INSPIRED MINDSET | 193

self-develop you are acting in the movement of "Life "or "Higher Self."

Be definite, precise and certain in everything that you do. Define a clear vision for your life, a vision for who you are and what you stand for. Define what is most important to you and develop and work from your strength. Something that you are really passionate about, that will inspire you, make you jump out bed every morning excited to begin each day; and use the tools that you've learnt here to be successful. Once other people see what you have, they will be attracted to you and want to have what you have.

Create your own way of holding yourself accountable and a way of measuring and monitoring that you are on track. In business these are called Key Performance Indicators or KPIs. These need to be practical, measurable things that you do on a daily basis that will help you to live a successful life.

Decide today to start to transform your life by developing habits that inspire your mind to help you create a successful life.

The following are my own practical habits or KPIs that I created for myself. I practice these every day and use them as measures to help me keep on track.

1. *I start everyday with gratitude*—I flood my consciousness every day when I wake up with so much gratitude, by reminding myself of all the abundance and goodness that I have in my life and thank my 'Spirit' for all the blessings and wonderful gifts in my life.

2. *Conscious awareness*—Because I understand the **SPAM** system and how the mind works, I am constantly managing my emotions and thoughts on a moment by moment basis. I am constantly listening to that inner voice and monitoring that it's in line and supporting me in everything that I am doing. Because I understand that thoughts are just tools, I watch how I am responding to situations or thoughts that I am having making sure that I don't assign thoughts the wrong interpretation or emotional weight, hence choose to act and respond appropriately.

3. *State Management*—I have a number of key states that I consciously choose to experience and act from on a daily basis.

   a) *Gratitude;*

   b) *Curiosity*—to ensure that I am open to new ideas and new ways of looking at situations;

   c) *Passion and excitement*—to keep me engaged, energetic and enthusiastic

d) *Discipline*-to ensure I follow through;

e) *Fun & Joy*—to allow me to be playful and enjoy whatever task I am undertaking, so that I look at it as an adventure;

f) *Smart*—To check that I am solution-focused, considered what's possible or have asked for help when I need it; and

g) *Honest*—To ensure that I am being real with myself and others.

4. *Exercise*—I make time every single day to exercise my body; whether it is walking briskly to the train station on the way to work or setting aside 30 minutes intensive exercise 3 to 4 days a week.

5. *Good Quality Nutrition*—I ensure that my body is filled only with good quality fuel; My diet consists of organic foods full of vitality and life. I follow a high protein diet and endeavor to keep my system as alkaline as possible and ensure that I keep myself hydrated by drinking 2.5litres of distilled water everyday

6. *Set daily outcomes* of things that I need to focus on, thereby activating my RAS to pay attention to and filter for opportunities. This alerts my consciousness to pay attention so that I recognize those opportunities when they present themselves.

7. ***Success conditioning***—I make sure that I run a mental movie just before I sleep each night of all the successes, however small that I have had that day. I visualize and play a movie of my life's vision every night before I sleep and every morning when I wake up so that I jump out of bed full of passion and excitement for the day ahead.

8. ***Pay It Forward***—I am mindful to ensure that I walk my talk. I endeavor to treat other people as I would like to be treated. That is, I say and do good things for myself and other people and act from that mindset. I strive to walk my life's path and encourage others to be the best that they can be. I use the tools I have learnt to be successful and as much as I am able, share those tools or my understanding with others so that they too are inspired to discover their own path and become the best that they can be and pass that on.

Decide today to start to build your inner presence. It is this that will draw other people to you.

The Higher Self, the Source, the part that gives life, the true self, they are all one and the same. This natural and inherent part of you is perfect, loving, intelligent, intuitive, sensitive, compassionate, and brave and wants the best for everyone.

Remember that, the nature and aim of the "Higher Self" is to evolve. It can only do this through the process of each of us developing the true "SELF" within each one of us.

It is a perfect, loving, abundant and intelligent Energy, whose aim is to give you everything that you want and make the best better. Therefore, it has a vested interest to ensure that each one of us awakens to our true nature by developing the true "SELF" within. The more you work in partnership with the Higher Self and help others to awaken to their true nature, the more success and abundance it helps you create. In other words, the more you pass on the "holistic mind-set system" or "Pay It Forward" through your behaviour and successes that you are having, the more your inner presence or true "SELF" will grow and the more abundance and success you will experience.

I have shared my KPIs with you, things that I do and measure on a daily basis to ensure that I am living from the holistic mindset and continuously growing my own presence. This is very easy to measure. All you need to ask yourself is one or two questions:

> *Am I following Life's vision? Or*
> *What have I done today to grow my inner presence?*

Now, it is time for you to develop your own measures or KPIs that will help you live a successful life. Are you ready for the adventure?

In this book, I have shared with you some tools and techniques and how I use them. This is my way, however I look forward to hearing about your own way and your own successes, because within you lies The Way.

THE INSPIRED ACTION YOUTH PROGRAM

My life's mission and purpose is to invest in our future generation. I am absolutely committed in the education of young people who are striving to become entrepreneurs to be properly equipped with the right tools in terms of a fit for purpose mindset and the right financial education. In society today, young people are in a crisis and many lack direction. Teenage suicide, drug abuse and violence have risen to epidemic proportions and we must invest in our future generation to reduce this trend.

The Inspired Action Youth Program is part of my commitment to make a difference in young people's lives—particularly in the youth of the African continent. Our Youth Program is centered on education and offering paradigm shifts by providing real practical skills, tools and strategies that can be applied to help young people be self-reliant by becoming entrepreneurs. Through business they can have role models who can positively influence the direction of their lives. In our attempt to encourage and inspire the next generation, especially those living in tough circumstances, the Inspired Action Youth Program is committed to investing its time and resources in providing financial education to young people. More than ever, young people especially in Africa need heroes. We will be reaching out to various communities and schools with a message of self-esteem, purpose and hope. A message that tells young people: "You can be and become in life whatever you choose to be." All you need is the right mindset, commitment, discipline and the right tools to take the right action.

Our program will deliver this message through role models that our young people can aspire to, including other successful entrepreneurs, sportsmen and women, business men/women and other local heroes. The Inspired Action Youth Program will bring this message of hope to various schools and community groups by speaking to young people directly and inspiring them to dream big and create a positive future for themselves. Imagine what kind of world we could have if all our youth were given the support, tools, training and encouragement they needed to become the best that they can be. If you would like to get involved and lend your support to the Inspired Action Youth Program, please email:

youthaction@inspiredactionacademy.com

ABOUT THE AUTHOR

Rebecca Bukenya is a certified Leadership and Business coach with over twenty years' experience working in corporate life in the financial services sector in the city of London. She is an entrepreneur, mindset coach, and founder of the Inspired Action Academy. She specializes in helping entrepreneurs, coaches, leadership teams, and small businesses implement effective operating structures and processes so that the businesses run successfully and profitably.

Born in East Africa, she grew up in the UK, where she currently lives. She has an excellent understanding of both African and Western cultures.

Rebecca believes that we are all capable of much more than we imagine. She has a deep interest in the humanistic aspect of life, self-expression, and the potential we all have to positively impact our own lives and the lives of those around us, to inspire and lead by example.

She has an in-depth understanding of human behavior and, in particular, how the mind is conditioned for either success or failure. Rebecca believes that having a solid foundation of the right mindsets is the key to creating a phenomenal lifestyle.

REFERENCES

Bandler, Richard and Grinder, John. *The Structure of Magic I: A Book about Language and Therapy.* Palo Alto: Science and Behavior Books, Inc., 1975. 6.

Chopra, Deepak. *Self Power: Spiritual Solutions to Life's Greatest Challenges.* New York: Random House, 2012.

Hill, Napoleon. *Think & Grow Rich.* Radford, Virginia: Wilder Publications, 2008.

Holmes, Enerst. *The Science of Mind.* Radford, Virginia: Wilder Publications, 2007.

Kilts, Professor Clinton, University of Emory, Georgia; Professor Paul Whealan, University of Wisconsin; Brown Foundation for Human Neuroimagery.

Pettus, Elise. "The Mind–Body Problems." *New York Magazine.* 14 Aug 1995. 28–31, 95. Also see Deepak Chopra, "Letters: Deepak responds," *New York Magazine.* 25 Sept 1995. 16.

Robbins, A. *Unlimited Power.* New York: Fawcett Columbine (Ballantine Books), 1987. (Neuro

Associative Conditioning or NAC is a system devised by Anthony Robbins to create permanent, lasting change.)

Wiener, Norbert. *Cybernetics, or Communication and Control in the Animal and the Machine.* Cambridge: MIT Press, 1948.

12166315R00125

Printed in Great Britain
by Amazon.co.uk, Ltd.,
Marston Gate.